Still Life with Cars

Still Life with Cars

An Automotive Memoir

JOHN L. LUMLEY

McFarland & Company, Inc., Publishers
Jefferson, North Carolina, and London

Library of Congress Cataloguing-in-Publication Data

Lumley, John L. (John Leask), 1930–
Still life with cars : an automotive memoir / John L. Lumley.
p.   cm.
Includes index.

ISBN 0-7864-2053-7 (softcover : 50# alkaline paper) ∞

1. Lumley, John L. (John Leask), 1930– 2. Automobiles—
Maintenance and repair — Biography.   3. Automobile engineers—
United States— Biography.   I. Title.
TL140.L85A3 2005   629.2'092 — dc22   2005013988

British Library cataloguing data are available

Front cover: The author's 1954 Armstrong Siddeley
Sapphire 346 after restoration.

Manufactured in the United States of America

McFarland & Company, Inc., Publishers
Box 611, Jefferson, North Carolina 28640
www.mcfarlandpub.com

Contents

Preface

I AM A PROFESSOR OF aerospace and mechanical engineering, but I lead a double life.

This is the story of my life with cars. It is sort of a dirty little secret, because I am supposed to be an intellectual, a university professor. Greasy fingernails somehow don't go with the image. I feel defensive, that I have to explain that cars are only a hobby, and that what I do for a living has lots of intellectual content. I am afraid that people's worst fears about what engineering professors really do will be confirmed. This is probably also a very American story, in the sense that for complex sociocultural and economic reasons it is most likely to have happened in the United States (the UK and various Commonwealth countries are also a remote possibility).

What I do for a living is somewhere in between applied mathematics and mathematical physics. It has a very long fuse. An idea that I have this year is likely to bear fruit some 20 years hence. I find my profession very satisfying, but it has two disadvantages—it is a mind game, and has no hands-on aspect, and it certainly has no instant gratification. I need in my life something that I can make with my hands, and something that comes to fruition in a reasonable length of time. Restoring cars involves many skills, and while it is demanding, it does come to an end in a reasonable length of time, and the finished product is very satisfying. It might be objected that I should do engineering experiments, which would be more hands-on. Half the theses I have supervised have been experimental; however, it is the student who gets to do the hands-on stuff, not me. The combination of doing cars at home and fluid mechanics at school has worked out very nicely for me, and I have even been able to combine them.

Inevitably, my life with cars has not been independent of my professional and personal lives: I was immersed in a world my parents made, I grew up, got married, had children and then grandchildren, got a job, got promoted, changed jobs, traveled and generally had a life like other people. But all the time cars were a part of it. It is impossible to tell you about the cars and what they meant to me without putting them in the setting of my life. So, you will hear about my job and my family and their cars as well.

Chapter 1

Mostly early recollections

W HEN I WAS A TEENAGER, and up to my elbows in grease, my father assured me that he had also worked on cars before I was born. Although he fabricated and fixed virtually everything around the house, from bricklaying to plumbing, wiring, carpentry, furniture making, plastering, tilesetting, gilding, and on and on (I remember a dog house he built that could have been rented to a lodger), in my recollection, he was strictly hands-off as far as the mechanics of cars were concerned. We worked together on many projects, and he taught me an enormous amount, and at the dinner table I learned a lot about the early days of cars. But we never worked on cars together. In fact, it is likely that his hands-on experience of cars was limited to adjusting the valves, but lack of experience never stopped him; he loved trying things he had never done before. There is no question that he was a car nut.

When the stock market crashed in 1929, he picked up a Hudson with a custom paint job that had been prepared for someone who had leaped from a window ledge. The car had a rubbed varnish finish in midnight blue, and artillery wheels. He was very proud of this vehicle, and every weekend we would wash and polish it. I was six and something at the time, and I was allowed to use the spoke brush to clean the varnished and pinstriped wheels. He was very particular about wiping down the paint with a carefully wrung-out chamois after washing. I remember sitting in the back seat on the plush velour upholstery with my feet dangling far above the floor.

As teenagers my parents had immigrated to the United States with their families around 1910; Mom from Edinburgh, Scotland, and Dad from Belper, in Derbyshire, England. They met here and married just after the First World War.

My earliest memories of my parents are from about 1934, when I was four and they were about 40 (I was born late). Dad was a relatively trim man of about five foot ten, with a brush moustache, dark hair and a very small birthmark in the middle of his forehead, which looked almost like an Indian caste mark. From time to time he would shave off the moustache or grow it back, and I usually did not notice. He was rather dapper, with a fairly formal manner. He was a perfectionist, and did an incredible job at whatever he tried.

All his life Dad had flat feet that hurt, and terrible teeth. I look superficially more like Dad, particularly about the face, and we are about the same size, but thank God I inherited teeth and feet from Mom's side of the family.

My mother was five feet and a proud quarter inch tall. She found the Hudson a trial to drive. Both steering and brakes were almost more than she could manage. I have still a clear recollection of kneeling on the back seat, peering in horror out of the back window, as we drifted slowly backwards down the steep entry ramp of a parking garage into heavy traffic in downtown Detroit, my mother screaming as she tried to exert enough force on the brake pedal to stop this disaster in the making. I don't remember the outcome, but the car was never damaged in my memory, so she must have managed to control it.

Mom was definitely not the fix-it type. She was a bright woman who had been a medical secretary before she married, and who would have done well in business. She had a fairly abrasive manner, tending to tell people exactly what she thought, perhaps acquired as the youngest of three sisters. This was a full-service, equal-opportunity family; she was equally abrasive to Dad and me, and we defended ourselves vigorously.

I was born in Detroit and lived my first couple of years there. We were back in Detroit again when I was between five and nine years old, and then again when I was in high school, 1944–1948.

Living in Detroit from time to time certainly had an influence on my love of cars. Without being conscious of it, men in Detroit were continuously aware of cars and of the industry, much more so I suspect than in other cities. It may have been true of women also, but I cannot vouch for that. Of course, Detroit is completely economically dependent on the automobile industry, and the times I remember involve the Great Depression followed by the Second World War, both of which had an enormous effect on the industry. Although executives in the automobile industry tended

A 1929 Hudson. Not ours, unfortunately, but very like it. Reprinted with permission from Conde, John A. 1980. *The Cars That Hudson Built.* Keego Harbor, Mich.: Arnold-Porter Publishing Co.

to socialize only with each other, it was inevitable that even people not directly involved in the industry would know a few people who were connected in some way, or would be indirectly influenced by decisions in the industry. Adults talked about what was happening at the Rouge plant, because it would influence business at the shoe store, or new construction. Teenagers, of course, were much more interested in the new models that were being produced.

When Dad and I went on errands on Saturday mornings, Dad often let me sit on his lap and steer. These outings usually involved detours to look at interesting things. Dad was an electrical and mechanical engineer who had worked at times for the electrical power industry, and at times for architectural firms, so we sometimes drove past electrical substations he had designed, and sometimes past buildings of architectural interest. These might have been ones that he had had a hand in, or ones that were simply unusual. Sometimes the object of interest was completely different. I recall one of the first "modern" houses, in what I now recognize as probably Bauhaus style (this was about 1935); he hated it, but we saw it and commented on it nearly every Saturday, because it lay on our normal route to do errands. This also sticks in my mind because this was a section of divided parkway, where I was allowed to steer.

I remember his taking me to see Raymond Loewy's new, streamlined design for a locomotive. Could this have been the Twentieth Century Limited? In any event, it pulled into a railroad yard somewhere in downtown Detroit, and a crowd of interested spectators gathered. He carried me on his shoulders so that I could get a good view. We discussed the design on the way home; he was not a fan of what was referred to as "modern design," so he did not much like it, but he thought it was important to see it. He was very conservative in most respects.

Dad always treated me very seriously in conversation. He had one party trick for kids, in which he made objects placed in the middle of a handkerchief disappear and reappear (I found out years later that this involved a false thumb, which would fit over the real one), but generally speaking he was not good natured or full of fun. Serious was the word. Mom was too, for the most part, although I remember her playing with me when I was probably four, sculpting Scotty dogs from clay and building complex structures from blocks.

My parents were difficult to love, demanding, critical and judgmental of everything around them. They had few friends, and liked it that way. Wherever they were, they did not really put down roots, but held themselves apart, aloof, like aliens just visiting the planet. This may be common to first generation immigrants, for whom the new country is not as real as the old. It is also possible that my parents' sociocultural preparation in the UK did not prepare them well to navigate in the US culture. Certainly there is something funny about Brit immigrants; in Australia they call them the "whinging Poms," which translates as "whining Brits," because they never stop complaining, criticizing and judging, and never fit in, just like my parents.

My parents did instill in me an admiration for competence and skill, however. They encouraged my interests from an early age. I remember being sprawled on the living room floor happily drawing an elevator when I was in about the first grade, and including the whole mechanism of cables and pulleys and a motor to lift it up and down; this created quite a splash, and my father wanted to know how I had known how to draw it. I had no idea.

As a young man, Dad had been fascinated with the automobile. Shortly before Dad came to the United States, at the age of 13, he was taken to Brooklands (in England) where the U.K. Cadillac distributor had arranged a demonstration for the press, to advertise the new concept of interchangeability of parts. Three new Cadillacs were driven to Brooklands, with the

The Dymaxion automobile (1933), designed by R. Buckminster Fuller (1895–1983). Courtesy of the estate of R. Buckminster Fuller, Buckminster Fuller Institute.

press and public (including Dad) watching. The cars were totally dismantled, and the parts placed in a large pile. The pile was well shuffled, and three cars were reconstructed from the randomly selected parts. The cars were started, and driven off. This was a revelation at the time, since early automobiles were assembled with a great deal of work by skilled fitters, to make the definitely nonidentical parts fit. Interchangeability involved making large numbers of parts to close tolerances, a new concept. As I was growing up, Dad filled my head with this and other stories: the establishment of screw-thread standards; the man who could hand crank a Marmon V16; the time he had an engine fire in Harvard square, and many more.

One morning in Detroit when I was six, we took a detour so that I could see Buckminster Fuller's Dymaxion car. Dad and Bucky were young men together in Detroit, and had known each other casually. Dad remembered Bucky's contagious enthusiasm for his designs for the Dymaxion house and car. He tried to explain to me the positive aspects of this new design, but it did not mean much to a six-year-old. I remember thinking it looked very odd.

When I was in kindergarten, we lived relatively close to the Ford estate. My parents were friendly with the estate manager and his wife, the Fausers, who had three children. Their youngest was a little girl who was my age, and in the same kindergarten class. Every now and then, we would spend a Saturday afternoon with the Fausers, who lived in the gatehouse of the estate. I was allowed to play in the estate garage. This must have been about 50 feet square, and had a wonderful turntable in the middle, so that 12 cars could be parked, four on each of three sides. The turntable was rotated by the chauffeur, who stood at the edge and pushed with his foot. I was allowed to amuse myself for hours pushing the turntable and spinning around.

One of the cars in the garage was a miniature racing car that had been made for William Clay Ford, son of Edsel and grandson of Henry, in 1936 when William was 11. I remember seeing it in about 1936, when I was six, so it had just been made. It was a perfect miniature Indy car, perhaps six feet long, with a real four cylinder engine, which seemed to my eyes to be just right for a child my size. The estate was quite extensive, and had a considerable road system, and William used the little racer to run around the estate roads. I was so envious, so covetous, so jealous, I could barely contain myself.

Weekday mornings I was delivered to school in the Hudson. As I progressed through the first three grades, I became aware that the other kids thought our car was pretty funny looking. This was now 1939. There was a certain amount of jeering to be heard on the playground at recess, when we played marbles and Red Rover. As an adult, I know that these high, square old cars had been for the most part taken out of circulation by this time, their crankcases holed with a sledge to prevent resale, or shipped to Jalapa to become jalopies. Dad finally bit the bullet, and went to buy a new (or newer) car. I remember his coming home in a fury, because he had been given $25 for his perfect, lovingly maintained Hudson. What he brought home was a one-year-old Lincoln Zephyr sedan in beige.

This, of course, was much easier for my Mom to drive. It always had blocks on the pedals, and there were always movable cushions to get her a little closer to the wheel. I remember her telling me that I must not go around the neighborhood telling people that it was a V12, because it would excite jealousy. That might have been true — our house was one my parents had bought at the beginning of the Depression, and had managed to hold on to through it all; we were probably now economically a bit above the rest of the neighborhood, which contained a policeman (who would not let the kids on his creeping bent lawn with underground sprinklers) and a shoe store owner.

William Clay Ford's midget racing car. Photographed at Ford's 100th Anniversary of Motorsport weekend, Henry Ford Museum, Greenfield Village, October 13–14, 2001. Photograph by Ron Kowalke, courtesy of *Old Cars Weekly*.

The neighborhood also contained the mistress of Gar Wood, a mover and shaker in Detroit at that time. My parents tried to explain the concept of "mistress" to me, but it was difficult to grasp. Gar Wood's mistress was a single mother, and I played with her kid. He showed me Gar Wood's present to his mom — a coffin-nosed Cord. I thought the headlights, which disappeared into the fenders courtesy of a crank on the dash, were wonderful. I begged him to be allowed to turn the crank, but he assured me that we would both be skinned alive.

However, the war was coming, and the Depression was ending. People had a little more money to spend, although of course cars would not be available again for some years. Within a few months, we had moved to Ravinia, an upscale bedroom community north of Chicago. Dad was on the road a lot, selling electrical switchgear, and when I wasn't in school my mom and I took the car to go explore the rather elegant communities scattered like pearls along the shores of Lake Michigan. I remember seeing for the first time what must have been Dinkytoy models of automobiles. This was 1940, and England was at war — they must have been what I now call new old stock.

A 1938 Lincoln Zephyr sedan, but not ours. This one appears to be English; note the right-hand drive and number plate. Otherwise, it is virtually identical. Reprinted by permission from Hendry, Maurice D. 1971. *Lincoln: America's Car of State*. Marquee book no. 8 in Ballantine's *Illustrated History of the Car*. New York: Ballantine Books.

I remember Saturday afternoons when we would drive to one of the communities along the lake that had a good movie showing. I would be in the back seat. I can still remember the look and smell and feel of the car. My excitement at going on a drive, going to the movies, and the thought of a possible ice cream soda after the movie was tempered with a certain dread. We had a deal: I must practice my multiplication tables on the way to the movie, to the satisfaction of the inquisitor (my mom) or we would turn around and go home without seeing the movie. I must have been very naive, because of course this never happened, yet I continued to believe in it. I am sure my parents were as desperate to see the movie as I was. My mom was always a movie buff.

I recall a minor problem with the Lincoln Zephyr about this time. This was one of the first engines with an aluminum cylinder head. However, the concept of year-round antifreeze with corrosion inhibitors had not yet been developed. It was probably time for a valve job — a fifth grader was not conscious of these things. I remember Dad coming home with a very long face, bearing the bad news from the garage. The cylinder heads could not be removed. Of course, many other cars had the same problem: the aluminum heads and cast iron blocks formed a battery, with the cooling solution as electrolyte, and the resulting oxides of aluminum (which occupy much more space than the original metal) filled the clearance around the studs, locking the heads into place. Eventually, a cutter was designed, like a long, thin hole-saw, that could be worked down around the studs to free the heads.

In the summer of 1942 we moved to Bethlehem, Pennsylvania. Dad had taken the train, since he was required there immediately. He would be managing an electrical instrument manufacturing company. Mom and I saw to having everything packed into the moving van, and followed in the car. The roads were empty, because of gasoline rationing. Several times cars honked at us, and my mom speculated that they were complaining at our profligate use of gasoline. We had extra coupons, I believe, because my dad had been required to be on the road selling switchgear.

We lived at the top of a serious hill, on the back road to the Bethlehem Steel plant. Another road entered from the right at the foot of the hill. Every winter 18-wheelers would jackknife on our hill in the middle of the night, as the drivers realized to their horror that there was a stop sign at the foot. They came pounding on our door apologetically at 3:00 A.M., to call for assistance.

One day, Mom and I had been somewhere, and we stopped at the gate to pick up the mail. For some reason, we both got out of the car. When we looked around at some slight noise, we saw the Lincoln Zephyr quietly gaining speed backward down the hill. I sprinted for it, and managed to get the door open, and get in the car, and get it stopped. This must have been a miracle, since it is otherwise a mystery how a seventh grader could find the brake pedal.

That same summer, I lied to Mom as we turned into the drive, claiming that Dad had let me drive on a few occasions, and asking her to let me put the car in the garage. I felt that my experience steering as a six-year-old might save me from being struck by lightening. Mom believed it, and of course I ran the car into a stone wall when I could not make the final turn into the garage. Fortunately, the speed was low enough that there was no damage. Mom very delicately asked me if I had varnished the truth a little, but I heard no more about it.

In the summer of 1944, we moved back to Detroit. Again, Dad went on ahead, and Mom and I followed in the car. The next year I learned to drive in this car, under my dad's tender ministrations.

I should say that Dad had lied about his age to enlist in the army for the First World War. He never saw action in Europe, but he finished the war as a captain of military police in Saumur. As he told me when I was grown, his primary duties had been to have a slug of cognac on arising, round up the whores to spend a night in jail whenever it was politically necessary, and spend the afternoons drinking sparkling Vouvray on the banks of the Loire under the willows with a French vineyard owner who had lost an arm in the war.

Perhaps as a result of this experience, Dad always liked running things and telling people what to do, and everything went smoothly as long as they did it. These traits served him well in the positions to which he finally gravitated: executive vice president of several architectural firms in the Detroit area. As a driving teacher for a 15-year-old these qualifications were perhaps less than ideal. We did not actually come to blows, but there was a lot of shouting. If we had ever worked on cars together, it would probably have been in this mode.

In retrospect I must say he taught me very well. Parallel parking presents no problems, and he taught me to avoid bad habits that I see every day on the roads, such as pulling right before turning left (or vice versa). Late in the learning phase, if we both had to go downtown on a Saturday, he would let me drive. Brave man. Having taught my own children to drive, I can imagine what he was going through. I can still remember his telling me that there was no rush, that we were not on a race track.

When it came time to take my driving test, I was so nervous I forgot to shift. I was not generally a nervous type. However, by this age I had acquired, from dealing with my parents, a finely honed terror of authority figures, who appeared to hold absolutely arbitrary, and potentially devastating, power over me. Maybe this is natural for only children. The cop who took me out brought me back, saying that my car handling was fine, but he didn't know how we kept a clutch in the car. In my state of fear-induced paralysis I wasn't sure what this meant. He did say that I would have to retake the test, but as long as I shifted, I would be fine. And I was.

Chapter 2

Adolescence

FROM THE TIME I WAS quite small I had been taking things apart, building things, and watching and helping my dad as he made and repaired things around the house. I always had a model airplane underway from about the third grade (although most of them did not fly successfully). In the fourth grade I sliced a corner of my thumb off in a joiner. I made birdhouses and radio cabinets and laid bricks and helped with wiring as I got older, and watched with fascination as Dad gilded picture frames and produced rubbed finishes. I was thoroughly steeped in manual skills.

When we moved back to Detroit, it was time for me to start high school. Fortunately, there was a good private school just a couple of miles from our house, which was then called the Detroit University School. It later became the Grosse Pointe University School, and finally the Liggett University School. This was the school that had been attended by the Ford children and many of the children of executives in the automobile industry. The Ford family had given substantial sums of money to the school to set up an exceptional program. What they had in mind was that the children of the automobile industry should have some hands-on experience of the trade. In fact, the children of the automobile industry would not touch the program with a barge pole.

A graduate student in sociology could probably write a thesis on why the kids of the automobile industry were so averse to getting their hands dirty. I suppose many of their fathers had been involved in the early days of the industry, when it would have been impossible to avoid dirty hands. However, the fathers had probably learned early on that people who had fun messing around with engines were not the ones that would earn a lot of money. It was the managers and organizers, the deal makers, who would succeed, and this was probably the attitude imparted subliminally at the dinner table. It seems to me, however, that the world cannot be run with only managers and unskilled workers; from somewhere we have to get clever engineers who love machinery and gadgets.

I, on the other hand, felt I had gone to heaven. I had had lots of manual experience at home, and I loved working with my hands, loved making things and fixing things and drawing. I happily signed up for a large fraction of what was offered: automobile mechanics, machine shop practice, mechanical and architectural drawing, and hand fabrication. Also on offer, which I did not have time to take, were aircraft engine mechanics and glider construction.

Samuel Beeler ran all these courses, an extraordinarily kind, friendly and knowledgeable man. He had a barrel chest and huge shoulders, and his neck was the same width as (or perhaps wider than) his head, which was topped with thick, black, curly hair. Kids are cruel to teachers who are perceived to be unable to cope. I never saw Mr. Beeler treated with anything but respect.

For auto mechanics we had, of course, Ford engines and chassis, which we dismantled and reassembled. Toward the end of my first year, Mr. Beeler (or Sir, as we always called him, as in "Why don't you ask Sir," or "See what Sir says") got hold of a World War I Liberty engine, a V12 aircraft engine, which the more advanced students happily tore apart. Although I never took the aircraft engine mechanics course, it went on in the same room, and I knew a kid who was taking it, so I saw the inside of this engine also. This was a World War II surplus radial engine (the war had just ended).

At about the same time, Mr. Beeler obtained a very large surplus diesel powered generator, which had a variable compression ratio and could be started on gasoline. I did not stay long enough to be involved in tearing that apart, but I mention it now because we were all impressed to see Mr. Beeler hand cranking the monster.

I should explain that the kids who took these courses were a small and despised minority. Most of us were not particularly athletic and did not go out for a major sport, like real guys. We were all on the general squad, which did calisthenics and played a little soccer. So, in addition to being greasy, we were also wimps. The auto mechanics and shop courses took place in the same outbuilding in which the football team dressed, and we often heard their unambiguously expressed opinions. After three years of this one of them asked me tiredly just why I was doing this. I was so startled, all I could think of to say was that it might come in handy some day. As a matter of fact, it has become part of my professional stock-in-trade, so my answer was not as ridiculous as it sounded at the time.

A large part of high school is teasing and derision (which we have learned from the Columbine incident, if we were not aware of it before). I was teased for many other things, and the fact that I could do everybody's math homework or write their English papers only made it worse. In fact, I did once write a paper for hire, but my work was instantly recognized, being far too good for the client. I got so much pleasure from the shop courses, however, that it more than made up for the teasing.

The rest of my high school experience was more or less normal. I was the editor of the literary magazine, probably because no one else wanted to do it, and (in an unrelated activity) I learned to set type from a California job case. We printed an occasional basketball program on the ancient press. Until a few years ago I still had my plane geometry book that had been cut nearly in half by a little snot in the printing shop, using the device for trimming stacks of paper.

One winter morning, another student and I went to pick up the magazine that had just been printed. We were allowed to take one of the school station wagons, Ford woodies that were used to transport the lower school kids. The roads were covered with black ice, and I was going much too fast. More than a block ahead, a car pulled out of a cross street but got stuck on the camber of my road and could go neither forward nor backward. I tried to brake, but discovered that this locked the front wheels, and I could not steer. The other driver and I had plenty of time to contemplate the upcoming accident. When I hit him, just in front of the driver's door, he spun around beautifully. No one was hurt, but neither car was drivable. The other kid and I agreed that we would tell the school and the cops that I had not been speeding, a bald-faced lie. I was much more worried about the school than about the cops. The assistant headmaster had a nasty temper, and was often seen disciplining members of the football team; I liked him but was scared to death of him. As it turned out, he could not have been nicer. Cynically, I suspect the car was covered by insurance, and he was probably delighted that he did not have an injured student or irate parent on his hands.

At school, my best friend Ron was the son of a lawyer. Ron was a skinny kid with glasses and a brush cut, like most of us. Our relationship was based entirely on a shared obsession with cars. We compared notes constantly, shared tips and sources of parts, and visited each other's projects, but we always worked separately.

Ron's father was probating the will of a small farmer who had died leaving not much but his land, which had been gradually surrounded by the sprawling eastern edge of greater Detroit. I suppose the land was worth something. The farmer had also left the remains of a Ford Model TT truck in which chickens had been roosting for years. My friend called me, to ask if I would be interested in having the truck for one dollar.

I was absolutely enthralled. For a wonder, my parents said it was OK, although my father always made a point of first being judicious, asking for all the details, and wanting to know my plans—presumably trying to estimate what he was getting himself into. Of course, I had not given the details a moment's thought, but how bad could it be?

Ron agreed to help extricate the truck from the chicken shed and tow it home from the farm. We had planned to get the truck to my house in daylight, since we had no lights on the back. In the event, it took us so long to extricate it from the earth into which the wheels had sunk, halfway to the hubs, that it was pretty dark by the time we were on the highway. The truck had solid rubber tires, and the kingpins and steering gear were extremely worn. Rolling down the highway, we tacked from side to side, as the great wheels flopped first one way and then the other. The truck also had no brakes to speak of, so that I was constantly in a sweat about running into the back of Ron's car, being hit from behind, or being seen by a conscientious cop. Amazingly, we got home without incident.

That winter, I dismantled the truck. I went through gallons of carbon tetrachloride. I brought all the engine parts into the basement and cleaned them there. The smell of carbon tetrachloride still makes me sick. Rebuilding engines is a very messy business at the best of times. For a first-time teenager it is a nightmare. Or, I should say, for those around him or her. My mother had fits about the state of my hands, my feet, the house, and the smell.

I discovered that I had a pretty good memory. I was too impatient to stop to put tools away, but my memory was good enough for me to remember where each tool was when I needed it. I could put all the car parts together in a pile, because I could recognize each one like an old friend. My messy workshop drove my father to distraction. At my present age my memory is still pretty good, but I have to put the tools away; Dad would be happy.

There was very little wrong with the truck, aside from great age and great wear. It was remarkably complete. Mr. Beeler had recommended that we all buy Dykes' Automobile and Gasoline Engine Encyclopedia, which I devoured. I gave my copy to a young friend in the early '60s, and I often wish I had it today, for reasons of nostalgia. Dykes, as we called it, contained many recommendations of use to rural car owners in the '20s, such as how to file bearing caps, how to scrape babbitt bearings, how to plug a hole in a water jacket (use a bolt and two large washers, with canvas soaked in white lead), and so forth. It was just the right book for the Model TT. Using Dykes, I did what I could for the engine without investing heavily in parts. I removed 20 years of chicken droppings from the body, but left it at that. I did not touch the suspension.

With the engine back together, it was time to start it. This was my first experience with cranking an engine. Dad gave me practical instructions intended to avoid a broken arm. I cranked for most of a day, at least in my memory. The engine would fire occasionally, just often enough to keep me interested, but it would not run. When I could not stand it any more, I walked down to the service station a couple of blocks away and made a deal with the kid who worked there. He showed up at the house a few minutes later with the tow truck, and pushed me up and down our street until, miraculously, the engine caught and ran.

At this moment, the local police cruiser pulled alongside. He wanted to know what I thought I was doing with an unregistered vehicle on the public road. Fortunately, I was only a few feet from our driveway. I explained the whole situation, and threw myself on his mercy. He let me off, on the condition that I agreed to remove the vehicle from the public road immediately. It stalled going up the drive, and the tow truck pushed me into the garage. That was the only time I was ever able to get it started.

Since we lived on a dead-end street, and our municipality only had two police cruisers, which I am sure were more urgently needed almost anywhere else, I can only assume that one of the neighbors had called the cops, annoyed by this circus we were providing for his entertainment.

Over the next few months I tried again and again to get it started, tinkering with the carburetor, the ignition, the valves, anything that seemed to have some bearing on the problem, absorbing every possibly relevant passage in Dykes. Things were not improving, and frankly I was getting sick of it. Even as a teenager I was not into instant gratification, but I needed *some* gratification. In retrospect, probably the compression was very low, and the carburetor (primitive at best) surely had badly worn jets. I did not yet own a compression tester, and I had been unable to find replacement piston rings. The spark from the ignition was probably very weak.

In the spring I was under pressure from my parents to get rid of it, and I was ready. Ron and I had been cruising the junkyards, looking for interesting things. Ron had better sources of information than I did. He was very secretive about his sources. Some of these junkyards had an interesting car or engine in a shed, or under tarps, in the back. The owner would have come across this interesting thing at some point, and saved it from the crusher in hopes of making a little money on it, or perhaps out of love for cars; some of the owners were old car buffs. The owners had to be approached delicately. These were unshaven, mumbling, shambling, profane men, old before their time, and they would not show their treasures to just anybody. Ron was very good at sweet-talking them. One day we saw an Auburn supercharged eight engine under a tarp. Another, we found a Duesenberg coupe with a chopped top in a shed at the back of a yard.

I felt that the owner of the Auburn supercharged eight might be receptive to the TT truck. I visited him, talking of a running TT, complete. He was interested. He offered me $25 for it, subject to approval, which I was glad to accept. My dad towed me down to the yard. The owner's face fell as soon as he saw the truck. "I thought you said it was running," he said. I assured him that it would run, but that we had towed it because it was not registered. Very reluctantly, he parted with his $25. I never went back to that yard.

I had begun buying tools. For my first basic set of wrenches and sockets, my dad took me down to a distributor located in between pawn shops on Grand River Avenue, in an area where machinists and mechanics down on their luck pawned their tools (a professional death warrant), and those on the way up bought them.

My dad advanced me the money for this first set of tools, and I paid off the loan by tutoring French at school. I was doing pretty well in French, and there were several kids in the year behind me who were not. Of course, I knew nothing about tutoring, and the kids were in academic trouble because of lack of application, something I could not cure. It was not a marriage made in heaven. They hated me (their parents had forced me on them), and I hated them. The arrangement lasted long enough to pay off the loan, but no longer.

Later, in the same area of Grand River where I had bought my tools, I bought in the pawn shops a set of micrometers covering bearing and piston sizes. I was not entirely happy with my purchase of one of these, and when I saw a much nicer one in one of the shops, I tried to take in the one I had bought and hock it, intending to buy the one in the window. The owner looked closely at the mike I showed him, asked me my name, and threw me out of the shop. It was some time before I realized that they accepted on principle only tools that bore the owner's name, and presumed that any tool presented with someone else's name had been stolen. This was my first experience of being viewed as a probable criminal, and it made a lasting impression.

Now, I needed a new project. A few miles from our house there was a fruit and vegetable stand at which we sometimes stopped for produce. Behind the stand was a derelict car that looked very interesting. I could not immediately identify it, but it turned out to be a generous two tons of 1932 Nash twin ignition straight eight five-passenger sedan, with wire wheels and the spares carried on the fenders. The man who ran the stand assured me and my dad that I did not want it. My parents were not quite ready for another dose of the same medicine, having just gotten rid of the TT truck, but I begged and pleaded. I had to guarantee that it would not interfere with my school work, that extreme cleanliness would be maintained, that the garage would be kept relatively neat, and so on. They finally agreed, and we went back to the produce stand and struck a deal. Again, the magic number was $25. A few years later there would be yet another car that I would buy for $25.

The car was delivered to our garage and I started dismantling it. While I worked tearing everything apart, I was doing research at the public library.

Every Saturday morning I had to go downtown to my orthodontist appointment, my French lesson and my piano lesson. In my mind it is always summer, and I am wearing a suit jacket with a flower in the buttonhole, even though I have only just finished my sophomore year in high school; it is 1946, and I am 15. Things were more formal then, and my parents felt that going downtown required dressing. The orthodontist's appointment and the French lesson both took place in the core of the business district. For the piano lesson I took the streetcar up Woodward avenue to the grounds of the Detroit Public Library.

After my piano lesson, I went next door to the Library Annex, in a Victorian mansion on the grounds of the main library. Here were the archives for all literature pertaining to the automobile (now the National Automotive Historical Collection). They had a wonderful collection of originals of all the promotional literature and magazine advertisements for each make of car, for various periods. For Nash in 1932, there was a lovely thick book, 8½" by 11" in landscape format, of beautiful art-deco ads: some photographs, many in black and white; but also high quality artwork of the cars in exotic settings, with Maxfield Parrish skies, lovely ladies in cloche hats and flapper dresses, with feather boas flung around their shoulders, elegant gentlemen with fedoras, palm trees, yacht basins, country homes; and the cars: gleaming, in dark, glossy colors, ever so slightly longer and lower than they were in real life. This was long before the Nash had become a small, relatively cheap car. Here it was a large, imposing, upscale car, intended for people of substance. I was due home for lunch, so my time was limited, but I spent perhaps an hour every Saturday drinking in this wonderful fantasy world, and imagining what I would do to my car.

Later, I also visited the downtown branch of the library on the way home, finding books with titles like *The Automotive Chassis* and *High Speed Diesel Engines*, which I devoured, even though some of them had no bearing on the restoration of the Nash.

When I arrived home by a succession of streetcars and buses, reality set in. In my greasy car clothes, I was removing years of grime, undoing rusty fasteners, washing parts in solvent, and measuring the damage that time had done. I found that the crank pins were seriously scored and egg shaped (although the mains were adequate), and the cylinders oval and tapered by a moderate amount. I had only read of these conditions, but here I had a prime example. In substantially more than half a century since then, and innumerable cars, I have never seen wear as bad. Only 14 years had elapsed since the car had been new — it seemed to me much more, because of the enormous changes in styling that had taken place. The odometer indicated a mileage in the neighborhood of 100,000, which was consistent with the age. The car had no air cleaner, which was certainly part of the problem. I also have no recollection of an oil filter. I wonder about the metallurgy at the beginning of the Depression, but it is also more than likely that the car had not been cared for.

When I had the engine block out of the car, it was time for me to be introduced to the machine shops. There were perhaps a quarter mile of machine shops in downtown Detroit that did nothing but regrind cranks, rebore blocks, recondition rods, and so forth. Since the war was just ending, new parts and cars had been essentially unobtainable for four years, so rebuilding and reconditioning were very popular.

Paying for this was a problem. My parents were very tight fisted, for good reasons. They also did not want me to take a job, because they felt that it would interfere with my schooling. They did not give me an allowance, either. I was on demand feeding; whenever I needed money I had to ask for it, and give a detailed explanation of what I planned to do with it and what effort I had made to comparison shop and otherwise reduce costs. Dad was generally in favor of the car project, since he thought it would be educational.

However, Mom was the accountant. Her father had died young, and she and her sisters had had to work to make ends meet. During the Depression, she and my dad had had a very precarious time. It is no wonder that both my parents were more than a little gun shy about spending money. Mom wanted from me constant projections of total costs, end results, delivery dates and so forth. At 15 it was hard to bear.

In negotiation, my parents and I decided on cheaper solutions to many problems. Some parts were unobtainable, and a certain amount of creativity was required.

Already SECOND LARGEST BUILDER OF EIGHTS!

Latest available registration figures reveal that since the introduction of the new Nash in June, Nash Eight sales have increased until only one builder of Eights remains between Nash and first place! Nash today is the one car with *all* the newest, finest features of modern motoring. Sound-proofed body and chassis! Synchro-Shift transmission! Silent Second! Synchro-Shift free wheeling (optional)! Twin Ignition! Automatic chassis lubrication! *Drive it.*

PRICES
$795
to
$2025
f.o.b. factory

NEW SOUND-PROOFED BODY AND CHASSIS NASH

An ad for my Nash from *Collier's,* October 17, 1931, p. 29. Courtesy of the National Automotive History Collection, Detroit Public Library.

When it came time to assemble the engine, the piston and ring assemblies seemed a bit tight in the bores, but what did I know? This was the first time I had ever done this. They had to be knocked in with a hammer handle, but that is not abnormal. Everything depends on an educated feel for the fit, which I did not have. They were in fact much too tight.

When the engine was back together and back in the car (after great difficulty, using a block and tackle suspended from the garage rafters—it is a wonder it did not bring down the garage), it was time to start it. The starter would not turn it over. This was ominous, but my friends assured me it was just a bit tight, and that pushing it was the way to go. Again, I called on the guy at the service station a couple of blocks away. He pushed me up and down Mack Avenue (rather than our little street, to avoid the angry phone calls of the neighbors). He advised me to let him get us up to speed before I let in the clutch. The engine never turned over. When he in the truck could clearly smell burning clutch facing (I had also smelled it, but had no idea what it was), he suggested that we stop and reconsider. In a state of extreme depression, I had him push me back to our garage.

Obviously, the engine had to come apart again. I had no idea what was wrong. This was the end of the summer, and school was about to start. I received an ultimatum from my parents, who could see that I was now totally fixated on the engine, if I had not been before. I was to stop this nonsense and concentrate on my school work. They would not tolerate anything that would have a deleterious influence on my performance in school. I begged and pleaded, to no avail. We finally reached a compromise: I could not work on the engine, but we would find a mechanic who would take it apart and find out what was wrong.

We found a very nice retired mechanic, but I was in a terrible emotional state. I could not tell my car-buddies at school that I had farmed out the job to a professional, that I could not handle it myself. I am afraid I kept very quiet about the fact that I was not working on the car, until I got it back.

The mechanic had a terrible time removing the pistons. The problem turned out to be the piston rings. The rings had been supplied with what are called expanders, which fit behind the oil rings to increase the pressure against the cylinder walls. The pistons had not been designed for expanders, and there was not sufficient room for them in the grooves. They were responsible for the excessive drag of the pistons in their bores. When the mechanic removed the expanders, everything was fine.

With the car back home, there was a better chance that I could keep this whole sorry episode under my hat. I was now allowed to work on it on weekends, if my homework was finished for Monday. The engine ran beautifully (with the exception of a single piston slap), but it leaked every possible fluid from every orifice. No one had told me about gasket compound and sealant. I asked around about this matter, and was advised to use Permatex Aircraft Type Sealant. This is an orange-brown liquid, about as thick as heavy cream, which sticks to anything it touches and is nearly impossible to remove, since it is impervious to most solvents. It never completely dries, remaining sticky and flexible forever. It is a wonderful sealant, but things that have been put together with it are nearly impossible to take apart. If you are not planning to take them apart again, this is not a problem. However, if this is your first experience with an engine, it is probable that you *will* have to take the assembly apart again, and it will be a mess. Of course, I took apart everything that leaked, and reassembled it with the Permatex Aircraft Type gasket compound. This solved the leak problem, but created later problems.

My Nash had a Bijur chassis lubricator. This is a system that feeds oil to a number of suspension points through tiny $5/32"$ brass tubing from a container on the firewall. The system on the Nash had a pump that was operated by changes in manifold vacuum. Of course, all the tubing on the Nash was plugged up. Bijur still exists, and the system was used on the Rolls-Royce and Bentley from the '20s at least through the '50s. It is also used to lubricate industrial machines like punch presses. However, it was no longer used on cars produced in Detroit. With great difficulty, I found a source for parts in a one-room office in a building across from the General Motors Building, containing two old men and a lot of filing cabinets—all that remained of the high hopes which someone had had for the success of the system on Detroit cars. The old men were quite bemused to see this earnest, stammering teenager asking for parts. In fact, they pulled from the back of a file cabinet 25 feet of tubing and a gift selection of fittings (for all of which I was not charged), and kindly asked me all about my restoration. I could not believe my good luck.

Dad was a bear about the brakes on the car, wanting strong assurances that that they had been restored to excellent condition. These were mechanical brakes, operated by pull cables and rods. Everything was worn and either buried in grease and dirt or rusted almost beyond recognition, but I managed to get it all apart and cleaned, and the worn parts replaced, lubricated and back together. Then I had to learn how to adjust mechanical brakes. After three or four tries, I managed to get them balanced perfectly. They really operated very well for the life of the vehicle.

Finding miscellaneous parts for the brakes and exhaust system required visits to various parts stores. New parts for anything were essentially unobtainable. Some new old stock parts were still around, but the majority of parts were used, and possibly reconditioned. One of my favorite places was Airport Auto Parts, in a densely populated, heavily industrialized, poor area of Detroit, close by a small airport, which may have been the municipal airport at one time. Large gas storage tanks were visible all around. This was a junkyard, but since land was at a premium, junked cars could not be preserved intact. A sort of triage went on in the yard — a surly guy with a lit cutting torch in one hand and an engine crane went over each incoming car, turning it on its side and cutting it up, sorting the pieces into two piles, scrap metal and reusable. Some nut-and-bolt dismantling must have gone on, but I never saw it. The reusable parts were taken into the building and sorted into great bins and shelves. The floors of the building were divided into narrow corridors flanked by these bins and shelves, rising to the ceiling, the corridors lit by a single, unshaded 40 watt bulb. The bins were labeled with things like "39 Chev RF," and in that bin you would find six or eight right front fenders for '39 Chevrolets; or perhaps "36 Ford V8," and the bin would contain a gift selection of transmissions for that car. I know this because I became such a pain in the neck, constantly asking for things that were probably unavailable, that I was given the run of the place to find my own parts, if I could. Often I could, not necessarily for a Nash, but from some other car; I had a good visual memory, and could carry in my head a fairly accurate idea of the size and shape of the part I was looking for, and I could sometimes spot a part that would work. When this did not pan out, the counter man was often a big help. Sol had one wandering eye, so that I could never tell where he was looking; when it seemed to be my turn at the counter and he asked if he could help me, I could never refrain from looking over my shoulder, where he seemed to be addressing another customer. He was a walking interchange manual, and could often identify a part from another car that would fit in my application.

The body was in relatively good condition, with virtually no rust and only a few dents. I do not know when municipalities started to put salt on the roads, but it was evidently much later. The sheet metal was extraordinarily thick, probably 18 gauge. I bought a hammer and dolly and worked my way around the body, doing more damage than good, attempting to remove the few dents. Then I thought I should paint the parts that had been subjected to my tender ministrations.

I bought a cheap spray gun of the type with an electric vibrator as an air supply, and a quart of lacquer, on the recommendation of the guy in the paint store. I knew absolutely nothing about this process. I had watched housepainters applying paint to the living room walls with a brush numerous times, but this was quite different. I knew that the surface should be sanded; asking in the paint store, I was advised about the grade of paper required. No one told me about wet sanding. I don't know whether body filler existed at that time, but I did not use any. I diligently sanded the left front fender, which had been straightened, and got out the spray gun.

The first coat went on not very well, with quite a few drips and runs; I was unhappy, but I felt I could probably sand out the drips after it was dry. As it dried, however, it lifted the paint beneath; that is, the paint bubbled and blistered. The car had been painted with enamel at some time (not at the factory), and enamel and lacquer are not compatible, which any idiot (but me) knew. I had no idea what the problem was. I removed all the new paint, and as much of the original paint as I could, and tried again. Of course, the same thing happened. I had no idea of how clean the surface must be.

This process continued through three or four coats, over the course of two days, until finally I started with a perfectly clean, shining fender. Then the paint did not cause anything to lift. Now I had to get rid of the drips and runs. By this time I knew about wet sanding, and I began to delicately sand down the problem areas. Of course, since I had only one coat on the fender, I immediately went through to the bare metal. I repainted. I tried sanding again. I went through. I repainted. This process continued for some time. Notice, incidentally: no primer. Since I had initially been applying the paint over existing paint, I had been told I did not need primer. Eventually, I got enough paint on the fender so that when I sanded I did not go through. I had been told that I should now use polishing compound, and I had bought some. I began to use the compound, and of course I rubbed through. Back to square one — repaint, resand, repolish. And so on. This process went on for the better part of two weeks. When I went back to the paint store for more paint, and told the guy about my problems, he was very sympathetic, and explained about the incompatibility between enamel and lacquer, and how I could have changed to enamel and simply applied it over the existing paint without a problem.

Eventually I got a coherent layer of paint on all the parts of the car that needed it, all drips and runs were sanded out, and the paint was compounded so that at least the sanding marks did not show. I cannot say that it was a high gloss. In fact, the new paint looked not much better than the original paint on the parts of the car that had been covered. At least, however, the car was a uniform color, and it looked as though somebody cared. More than that I cannot say. The whole experience had been a nightmare, and I was happy to be done with it.

Tires were a problem. They were available, but they were expensive. Considering the size of the wheels, only truck tires would fit. This meant negotiating with my mom again. I argued that without the tires, all the previous investment would be wasted. We got the tires. Something needed to be done to the wire wheels. They had been chromed, but the chrome was long gone. I was for painting them with aluminum paint. Dad counseled against it, saying that it would look like a cheap, homemade job. I went ahead and did it anyway, on the grounds that there were few choices. It was quick and easy, and would probably not look too bad. Of course, he was right, but I managed to ignore the fact.

I started to drive the car back and forth to school, and to use it to run around Detroit looking for parts. I was once asked to give someone a push when his car stalled in heavy traffic and would not restart. I was thrilled. The car behaved beautifully and was a pleasure to drive. Although the steering was pretty heavy, it was not a problem for a teenage boy. Several times I drove carloads of kids from school to "away" football games, although I was not a real football fan. I was attracted not by the game, but by the idea of being the guy with the car who could provide the transportation. The engine was a low speed, high torque design, so that it could be taken down to idling in high gear, at perhaps a couple of miles per hour, and floored; it would pick up smoothly to cruising speed without hesitating. This also had to do with the twin ignition, which meant that it almost never misfired. Cruising through Detroit traffic, I also practiced shifting without using the clutch. My recollection is that there was no synchromesh, so that speeds had to be matched before engagement, with or without a clutch.

I was in serious need of money. From time to time I dropped into the Nash dealership that gave me the large discount, to buy one or another part for the Nash. On one visit, the counter man asked me if I would be interested in rebuilding the engine of his car. What a rush! I had suddenly become a professional! And, I had an opportunity to earn serious money. Of course, I said yes. I carefully calculated a price, which he immediately accepted. I should have been suspicious. He delivered the car, and I started. It turned out that he expected work that I had not counted on, that involved substantial charges at the machine shop; to make it worse, his expectation was quite reasonable — I had just not been thinking. In addition, I had undervalued my time seriously, so that in the end I was essentially working for nothing. I felt that to stop work and demand a renegotiation would be unprofessional, especially since the situation resulted from my inexperience. I did a beautiful job on the engine, but as it moved toward completion I got madder and madder, as it became clear that I would take nothing home from this job. My client, however, was delighted.

My Nash had vacuum wipers, and these would simply stop on hills or during acceleration. One of my car magazines recommended a vacuum storage tank to avoid this problem. I made one, using a large flat-sided tin can that had held some food stuff, perhaps a gallon of olive oil. The fabrication was complete, but the tank was not installed when it was time to leave for school. I took the tank with me and installed it in the school parking lot, surrounded by my car-buddies. My mom would definitely not have approved of this mixing of business and pleasure. The installation complete, a couple of minutes before the first bell, leaving the hood open I started the engine to test the tank. My audience began to giggle, and then to laugh uproariously. I shut off the engine and got out of the car to find that the tank was now neatly collapsed to zero volume. Then the bell rang, and I had to leave to deal with this humiliation later. This was an object lesson in the power of atmospheric pressure. I later replaced the can with something much more robust, which was very satisfactory.

One day, when I pulled into a parking place in the school lot, there was a strange clunk that I could not identify. I was late for class, however, and did not have time to investigate. During the afternoon, I was in drafting class when a small delegation of my classmates came in, carrying something covered with a cloth. They were trying to contain laughter, so I suspected some sort of teasing. When they uncovered their prize, however, it was revealed as the right-hand side of my transmission, which had fractured and fallen off into the snow underneath the car. I was aghast, and speechless, as they stood there laughing their heads off.

Now I had to find another transmission. This required a full-scale search of all the junkyards in Detroit. I finally found one that would fit from an earlier model at Grand River Auto Parts. This was an enormous multi-floor frame building of the Victorian era, which must have been a light manufacturing facility when it was new. It had a small yard in the back, where cars were dismantled as they were at Airport Auto Parts. Inside the building, however, the focus was a little different from that at Airport.

To begin with, they had the first degreasing tank I had ever seen: this was a tank about four by six feet. The tank and solvent were heated. At the top of the tank there was a chilled water pipe to condense the vapor and send it back to the tank, and above this was a three-foot-high screen to make sure the solvent vapor did not escape. This meant that the rim of the whole affair was perhaps eight feet above the floor, so that to peer in you mounted a small stair and stood on a platform. There was a wand, allowing the operator to spray the part with solvent. Having spent untold hours laboriously cleaning grease and muck off parts with various scrapers, rags and solvents, I found this tank quite wonderful. The transmission I wanted had been still out in the yard, under the snow; the inspection plate had been removed, and there was ice inside. It was lowered into the tank, and it began to reappear magically as the heat and the solvent melted and removed everything extraneous.

In rooms on the upper floors, workmen dismantled and made some effort to recondition various parts that came in. This reconditioning was pretty rough and ready; I saw a man with an air-driven disk sander trimming the edges of a badly worn steering worm, for example. When finished, I am sure it would be adequate, but no better. However, since these were the only parts that were available, they were much in demand.

I took my precious transmission home. My own gears were better than the ones in the new case, so I swapped them, and installed the transmission in the car. It was wonderful.

This was the spring of 1947, and I had just finished my junior year in high school. As a graduation present, the parents of one of the seniors gave him a little red MG. A friend and I were standing on the steps of the school after lunch when he brought his toy around to be admired. This was one of the wealthier and more obnoxious of the seniors, and certainly not a friend of mine, but the car was so wonderful that I shamelessly made up to him in hopes of being allowed to see the engine. I was in love. I had never seen anything like this. The only cars I had worked on were large, relatively unsophisticated Detroit products. The MG was like a Swiss watch. Its engine sounded like a sewing machine. It seemed almost too small for an adult — more like a toy for a wealthy child. I wanted one in the worst way.

I would, in fact, have the care and feeding of an MG a couple of years later. In the meantime, however, I had to take care of my Nash. During the spring of my senior year, one of the rear axle shafts broke. By diligent searching, I managed to find another axle shaft, and we were fine for a while.

My adolescence was coming to an end. I felt under a lot of pressure to make some serious decisions about my life. What was I going to do, where was I going to go to school?

I had done very well in high school. When the representative of Harvard University came around looking for likely people, I was awarded the Harvard Book Prize. This was taken to indicate that Harvard would welcome an application from me. So, I decided to go to Harvard, even though I still wasn't sure what I wanted to do in life. Needless to say, I was accepted. Incredibly, I hadn't applied anywhere else. Mom was sure that it was a hotbed of communists, and that it would be extraordinarily expensive.

It was now almost time for me to go off to Harvard. At the end of the summer, a week or two before I left, my parents asked me to rebuild the engine of our Chevy, which had been bought just before the war. I was happy to oblige, and did a complete job on it: rebore, regrind, pistons, pins, rings, shells. For a change, everything went without a hitch, and I went off to my first year at school feeling pleased with myself.

Chapter 3

Freshman year

I HAD BARELY SETTLED into my freshman dorm, completed registration, and begun classes, when I got an anguished phone call from Mom, asking if I had any idea why there should be water in the oil and oil in the water of the engine I had rebuilt. I was floored — this was not good news. I had evidently done something terribly wrong, but I couldn't imagine what. The usual reason for this condition is a blown head gasket, but since the head gasket was new and had been installed absolutely by the book with the most excruciating care, it seemed extremely unlikely. I explained all this. I did not hear for a week or two, and I had nearly forgotten about it, when I got another call, explaining everything.

My parents had a very clever mechanic whom they had used for decades. He was not fancy, and usually worked out of a one-bay shop. His body was curiously bent from arthritis and a lifetime of contorting himself to fit into cramped places. His most important characteristic was his intelligence. He could usually diagnose a problem when no one else could. This was the man whom Dad had paid to examine the brakes on the Nash, to make sure they were safe.

My parents took the ailing Chevy engine to him, and he kept it for a week, looking at it every day until he finally figured it out. It turned out that I had twisted a tiny oil line that ran through the water jacket so that it had ultimately fractured. When he replaced the line, everything was fine. However, I had to pay for the mental anguish, loss of use and general aggravation by enduring a blistering phone call.

I majored in engineering sciences and applied physics, the closest that

Harvard came to engineering. I thought I would probably become an automotive engineer, although this was subject to weekly change. I still was considering medicine and architecture in a half-hearted way.

In Cambridge, I was a fish out of water. I was bright enough, but a very emotionally immature 17, and not very socialized. I had been brought up essentially alone by parents who were antisocial and disapproving of most things. Aside from school work, all I knew was cars. Since most of us didn't have cars, this expertise was not much use. I was fairly abrasive, but I found a few friends. I drank a lot of beer, and got up too late for class, but managed to stay in school because I had been very well prepared in high school. For the first year, I stayed more or less away from cars. There were only two minor incidents.

One of my freshman roommates, who was from the Back Bay area of Boston, had a Ford V8 that needed to have its engine changed. He recruited several friends one night, and we descended on his family's back yard. We worked fairly diligently, and had all the auxiliaries removed, the various lines disconnected, the engine mounts unbolted and the drive shaft disconnected by about 10:00. His mother appeared with refreshments. Then we connected the chain hoist, expecting that the engine would pop right out. Nothing moved. We pulled harder; the whole front of the car came up. It was clear that we had forgotten to unbolt something, but there was nothing evident. We went over the engine with a fine-tooth comb. We tried again (on the grounds that perhaps something was frozen with rust) with the same result. I finally remembered from auto shop that there was a bolt hidden inside the water pump on each side, connecting the engine to the mounts. We disconnected that, and the engine came out. I was a celebrity for Andy Warhol's 15 minutes.

Another friend was also an old-car buff. Of course, in the freshman dorms, no one knows anyone else very well; "friend" is a relative term. This was someone I had seen a few times over half a semester. However, we liked each other, and he had bought a Hupmobile, something like a 1925. This had a large body shaped a bit like a stagecoach, with bulging sides, a flat roof, and a tiny hood in front. It was in rather nice condition, and was painted a pale blue. I thought it was charming. He wanted help with the carburetor, which badly needed cleaning.

Our efforts took place in a floodlit used car lot at night just off Massachusetts Avenue in commercial Cambridge, the only accessible place with enough light to permit working at night. I had cleaned the carburetor of my Nash using Drano. This is lye, and is extraordinarily dangerous to both parts and operator. It is permissible for steel parts, and will certainly remove all trace of grease and grime. However, for parts that are zinc alloy die castings, it is not a good idea. For reasons I do not now understand, I had had no trouble with my carburetor. The Drano had done a great job cleaning it, without the slightest damage. Perhaps it had to do with the composition of the alloy and the presence or absence of impurities. In any event, when we subjected the Hupmobile carburetor to the same treatment, and lifted it from the bath, we found it as full of holes as a Swiss cheese.

I was appalled. We were both appalled. I was nearly speechless. The carburetor was absolutely ruined, with no hope of repair. My friend was very quiet. I am afraid I stumblingly apologized and fled. I tried to avoid him for the rest of my time at Harvard, and I am sure he had no desire to see me. Only God knows how he managed to find a replacement carburetor for such a rare car, or what he did if he was unable to find one. I saw him at our twenty-fifth reunion, and we laughed about the incident. Maybe he has forgiven me.

The summer following my freshman year, I was very short of money, and took a job at the Chrysler Kercheval plant, working on the production line. My parents were not pleased. At Christmas, I had worked in the drafting room at the architectural engineering firm where Dad was executive VP. The pay was not wonderful, and although the work was satisfying, I did not really like working under the watchful eye of my father, whose office had a huge picture window looking out over the drafting room, the better to spot people who were schmoozing. The pay on the production line was essentially the best in Detroit for unskilled work, the result of union efforts. I would not have to join the union for three months, by which time I would be long gone.

Directly across from the factory was a residential street, and the residents sold space on their lawns for parking on a weekly basis. It was just a short walk halfway down the block to my car. I was driving the Nash back and forth to work. From my family's point of view, this was not appropriate work, or an appropriate environment, for a Harvard undergraduate.

Two of us, with long hooks, hauled the car bodies off the elevator, on which they had come from the paint line. We hauled them about a car length to a platform where they were inspected by two men with bright lights and grease pencils. Nearly invisible imperfections were picked up and marked. The bodies were sent either to the start of the production line, if they were perfect, or to the repaint line, if there was a paint problem. If there was a tiny ding, such as might be caused by a tool hitting the surface, the body was sent to a clever little man next to the inspection platform. In between bodies, I loved watching this guy. He had a collection of long steel rods with loop handles on one end, and right-angle bends on the other, with sharpened points on the ends. These would be snaked in between panels until the pointed end was in just the right place; he could tell where the end was by twisting the handle gently, causing the point to raise the panel slightly, changing the reflection. When the point was just under the ding, he would give the handle a strong twist, and usually the ding would completely disappear the first time. Sometimes it required a second iteration. Usually the paint was not damaged, and the body could go directly to the beginning of the production line.

All this took place around the repaint line, which disgorged repainted bodies to the beginning of the production line. The end of the repaint line was a gas-fired oven surrounding a moving line, so that the bodies were pulled through the oven to bake the enamel. The ambient temperature here in a Detroit summer was 130°F, and the union required that we get 20 minutes off each hour and that salt tablets be available at the water cooler. When I left the factory at night, my face was gritty with salt. The only place for us to go during our 20 minutes was the men's room, which had windows looking out on Jefferson Avenue where the street car tracks went by. Everybody hung out the second-floor windows hoping for a little cool air, smoking cigarettes, talking and commenting on the passing scene. I discovered that some of my colleagues were working two shifts in order to make house and car payments and buy washing machines and the like. These guys were like zombies from chronic fatigue. The work force was variable: there was a core of regulars, and a fringe of impermanent people. The latter were essentially vagrants. They would work for a few days to get a financial stake, and then disappear, presumably to consume their earnings. There was always a line at the hiring hall, and each morning the company hired the number needed to fill the vacant slots.

After a few weeks, I was promoted to the production line. I was responsible for putting the rubber strip on the bottom of the right-hand front door. I had a gun attached by a hose to a 50 gallon drum of trim adhesive, and I was supposed to squirt a line of adhesive onto the rubber strip, release the gun (which hovered on the end of a spring-loaded line from the ceiling), place the strip in position with my left hand, and reach inside the door with my right hand and bend four steel tabs over to hold it in position. I could, of course, reverse the hands, depending on which way I wanted to face. The first few hours were fine, but the ends of my fingers began to get very sore, and each successive bend of a tab was more and more excruciating. Changing hands was a blessed relief, but did not last long, since the other hand rapidly acquired the same problem. By the end of the shift, both hands were nearly useless. In addition, the trim adhesive from the gun was everywhere, no matter how careful I was. Everything

I had on was covered. I figured I could never survive another day without some help, so that night I designed a false finger-end out of steel strapping and masking tape, and I was home free. No more pain.

One morning on the way to work, the axle broke, and I had to park my car in a gas station for the day and make arrangements to have it towed home. This time I was not so lucky. I went to all the junkyards I knew about, again going as far south as Toledo, and could find nothing. In desperation, finally, I had the shaft welded. The welder said that it would not last, since the shaft around the break was crystallized, but I had very little choice.

Toward the end of the summer, I quit my job, having earned what seemed a princely sum. To my parents' horror, I wanted to buy a motorcycle with some of my funds, to take back to school with me. After what the State Department calls "frank and open discussions," we decided that I could buy a small motorcycle, and that Dad would come with me to make sure he approved. We settled on a used Royal Enfield, which I had never heard of, but which appealed to my dad. It had only four horsepower, but I had no desire for something like a Harley or Indian. I thought the Royal Enfield was lovely: it was relatively light and easily manhandled. The headlight and gas tank were badly scratched and needed to be repainted.

As my final project in machine shop practice in high school, I had made an air compressor. For hours I had cut cooling fins on a big chunk of cast iron, and bored it out. Finally I had it professionally honed, and made a double-acting piston. For bearings, I got two connecting rods from the junkyard and cut them off, using the wrist-pin bearings for the compressor's crankshaft bearings. The crankshaft was

My motorcycle and I at the end of the summer between my freshman and sophomore years, posed in front of Mom's flower garden. Just out of the picture on the left is the area of the driveway where I painted it.

not balanced or counterweighted, but it was adequate. With a war surplus oxygen tank as a receiver, it worked very well.

I bought a spray gun, and proceeded to get involved with paint again. This time I went straight to enamel, and I did use primer. Again, it was terribly discouraging. If the paint did not run, it was not shiny. If I got it shiny, it ran. With enamel, you cannot sand out the runs and compound it. You have to get it right the first time. I had no source of advice, although the solution was fairly simple. After four tries, stripping everything back each time and starting over, I managed by trial and error to get it shiny without drips. It was beautiful. I still am thrilled by a nicely done fresh paint job.

Chapter 4

Sophomore year

I WENT OFF TO MY SECOND year with the motorcycle. It was wonderful. I rode it everywhere, particularly to places where there were no legal parking spaces, which was most of Cambridge. I carried my roommates on the back. Once, my roommate assumed that I was turning right, whereas I was going to turn left. As a result, I leaned left, and he leaned right, and the bike did not turn. We went into the back of a parked car. Fortunately we were not going very fast, and no serious damage was done. Another time, we were coming back across Boylston Street bridge from a rather well-lubricated football game; I went a bit close to the cop directing postgame traffic at the Memorial Drive–Boylston Street intersection, and as I passed, he snatched my roommate off the back of the bike. I was blissfully unaware of this, and returned to Eliot House, parking the bike and going upstairs to our room before I noticed that my roommate was missing. The cop let my roommate go with a talking-to, and he showed up a few minutes later.

I used to ride the bike in the space between the curb and the first lane of traffic. This was a wonderful way to beat Boston traffic, until the day that someone opened his passenger door just in front of me. I survived that also, but I was shaken. Another time I was tootling along enjoying the weather when I looked up to find that the streetcar I had been following was now stopped to take on passengers just a few feet in front of me. I threw the bike sideways and brought it to a stop with the footrest nearly on the cobbles, just in time.

In Boston, the subways stopped running at 1:00 A.M. The legitimate bars closed at midnight. The bike provided transportation allowing several

35

of us to go down to Charleston near the navy yards, where an after-hours bar operated as a speakeasy. We knocked on the door, and a panel slid open; a very jaundiced eye surveyed us to determine whether we were too drunk to behave ourselves, and usually let us in. We used to ride four on the little Royal Enfield on the way down and back on these evenings out: I was on the seat; I had installed a long leather buddy seat behind (covered in yellow deerskin from a deer my dad had shot), and two roommates sat on that; and another sat on the gas tank in front of me. We did not make much speed, but the bike was maneuverable, and we were never stopped. Who knows how many south Boston Irish cops had a good laugh when they saw us. Sometimes, we would run out of gas on the way back to Cambridge. The gas consumption was not high, and just a little would be enough to get us back. I discovered that the gas remaining in the pump hoses of a closed gas station was more than enough.

But I am getting ahead of myself. Early in the year, there was a political rally in Somerville. I was there with a roommate. One of the cars in the parade, carrying a sound system and posters for the candidate, was a 1929 Chevy. We felt that we needed a car. That is, we felt that we couldn't take out a girl on a motorcycle, or, at least, if we did, our opportunities would be severely limited. We felt that this car might be in our price range, and we made an offer to the startled driver, a cheerful kid from south Boston, about our age. He was prepared to sell for $25. We formed a consortium of five kids, each contributing $5. I was the designated mechanic.

I found that the engine needed considerable work. To work on the engine, I parked the car in front of Eliot House with two wheels on the sidewalk, so that I could slide underneath in the gutter. This provided plenty of working room.

I should explain that the Harvard "houses," in which undergraduates live after their first year, are residential colleges, each with its own dining room and library. These were built with a massive donation at the beginning of the Depression by a man who had wanted to give the money to his alma mater, Yale, but had been refused. They are magnificent in conception and execution, beautiful neo–Georgian buildings constructed with no expense spared, and should have been intimidating. The idea of carrying out engine work in the gutter in front of one of them should have made us quail, but no one raised an eyebrow, so far as we were aware.

When I graduated, I needed recommendations, and one from my housemaster in particular. He was John Finley, a distinguished classical scholar. The housemaster and his family lived in a residence attached to Eliot House, and had a few house residents in for dinner every evening all year. Our engine work had been carried out proximate to his front door, so he had not been entirely unaware. Trying to find something memorable to put in my letter of recommendation, this was about all he could come up with, but he admitted that he did not quite understand just what I had been doing.

The engine had a badly cracked head, which needed to be replaced. Other than that, we put rings and bearings in it. Taking up a collection from the consortium to pay for these repairs made dealing with my mother seem like a piece of cake. The car also had a broken front spring leaf. We located an alcoholic mechanic on a side street off Central Square who was prepared to fix this at a price we could afford. He gas-welded the leaf, eyed it judiciously as it cooled from cherry red, and at what he judged to be an appropriate moment, threw a bucket of cold water over it. It was fine as long as we kept the car, perfectly tempered.

Next door to this mechanic was a junkyard. I was still compulsively checking every junkyard, hoping for an axle for my Nash, which still had the welded repair. For a wonder, the proprietor showed me a Nash one year earlier than mine, which had the same axle. He said that he would be dismantling it in a few days, to separate it into usable parts and scrap, and would save the axle for me. I should check back at the end of the week. I could think of nothing else all week; on Saturday, when I went back and asked the proprietor, he smacked his forehead and called himself stupid. He had completely forgotten, and the axle had gone to the scrap dealer. I was devastated — I felt this was probably the last axle I would hear of, and that proved to be true.

While we were there, we were shown a new arrival that seemed to the proprietor too good to cut up. This was a rather elegant short-coupled La Salle sedan from about 1930. It was complete and undamaged, and was uniformly covered in dust as though it had been in someone's barn for a decade, always a good sign. The proprietor tried hard to make the sale (he certainly knew the way to my heart), and the price was right, but our consortium was in no position to take on another car, and it would probably have required a lot of work.

One problem with our Chevy was the insurance. Massachusetts did not have state inspection, but the insurance company had the right to have its agent inspect the vehicle. Although the insurance was issued at the time of registration, it was provisional until the inspection had been carried out. After our vehicle was registered, the agent of the insurance company began calling our room, trying to make an appointment to see the vehicle. I was the owner of record, so the agent always asked for me. We were all primed to say apologetically that I was out, that no one knew just where I had gone, or when I would be back, but that we would be delighted to take a message.

The poor man never did connect, and we remained insured until we got rid of the car.

The car served us very well, providing transportation on dates at Wellesley and other local colleges, permitting us to go out to road houses on Route 9, otherwise inaccessible, from which we raced against the clock to get the girls back to their dorms before the curfew.

We also drove down to the Harvard–Yale game played in New Haven that year, and got back without incident.

We even drove to New York City to a cocktail party in an apartment on Sutton Place given by the mother of one of us. It is unbelievable, but I think we simply parked on the street in front of the apartment building. The mother was disgusted with us, since we all had far too much to drink, and one of us threw up in the bathtub. We drove back to Cambridge the same night, leaving directly from the party, none of us in a condition to drive. I could navigate pretty well on the parkways by keeping my eye on the curb and trying to maintain my distance from it. This worked fine until we passed a soldier on leave, trying to hitch a ride standing just about where my right front tire would pass. I was on autopilot, and the last I saw of the soldier was his startled jump for safety as he realized that our car was not going to swerve to give him room. A little later, our headlights went out without warning. One minute, lights, and the next, complete blackness, made worse because our eyes had no time to adjust. On large stretches of the Sawmill River and other parkways in New York and Connecticut there were no street lights, and at that hour of the night there was very little other traffic. If the lights went out on a straight stretch it was not so bad, but if they went out on a curvy stretch (of which there were quite a few just north of the city) it was very hard to tell just where the road was. I got out and fiddled with the wiring a number of times, until I evidently randomly found the problem, because it did not happen again.

Maintenance of the Chevy was a continuing financial problem. The insurance situation was probably going to come to a head soon: we thought the company would probably cancel the policy if they could not inspect the car, and it was unlikely that it would pass if it were inspected. Summer was coming, and no one wanted to keep the car over the summer. So, reluctantly, we sold it.

At about this time I was engaged in an escalating war of attrition with my mom over my spending. I mention this now, because it will have a bearing on my life with cars, as we will see later. Mom felt that I was spending too much, and she wanted a detailed report of what I was spending it on. Of course, I did not want to give such a report, since I would have had to admit that it was being spent on beer, cars and breakfasts bought outside the dining hall system because I had overslept. Both of us were becoming very angry. It was a bit like the Israeli–Palestinian conflict, with each side retaliating against the last indignity with an escalated new indignity. It reached a peak when I received a registered letter. I presumed this contained an excoriating dressing down and a set of new ground rules. I say "presumed," because in an inspired bit of daring I refused delivery, and had it returned to sender. After this, there was an ominous silence from home, but these things never go away, and there were to be consequences.

At the end of the year, the crankshaft in the overworked motorcycle broke. It is a tribute to its makers that it put up with our abuse for so long. As I was leaving at the end of the year, I took out the engine, dismantled it, and degreased everything with a proprietary preparation called Gunk, which emulsified the grease and was then washed off in the shower of a friend's room. I packed the engine in a suitcase and went home for the summer, leaving the motorcycle frame in the bike rack in front of Eliot House.

When I arrived home, the first thing I did was go to look at my beloved Nash. It wasn't there. I ran back to the house in great distress. Mom said that it had been sold to an itinerant junk dealer. I was devastated. I have never forgiven my parents, although I have tried hard to understand the situation.

In retrospect, they probably had several reasons. We lived in a neighborhood that, while rural, might have been described as upscale. Down the street from us was a minor vice president of GM; he was encouraged to buy a Cadillac or Oldsmobile from GM at a discount every couple of years, and we had a deal with him to buy the discard. I think my parents felt that a derelict car in the back yard made the place look more like Appalachia, and would eventually excite comment from the neighbors. I had carefully parked it at the back of the property behind a screen of trees, where it would not be readily visible, but this was probably a factor anyway. My parents were always very concerned about the opinion of the neighbors.

In addition, my parents did not accumulate anything. We were the only people I knew whose basement was entirely neat and clean, with no boxes of junk in the corners. The concrete floor and walls of our basement had been painted in two-tone colors like an industrial corridor. When I had been working on the Nash, I had wanted to save the rejected parts, sure that they would be useful someday. My parents exerted strong pressure to get rid of them, on general principles. I managed to fight a successful rearguard action, and saved a single neat box (that had been my toy-box when I was four), containing the parts that I thought might be most useful. I am sure that the presence of the Nash in the back garden was a continual annoyance.

Probably most important was our guerrilla war over money. I think it is quite possible that the selling of the Nash was a retaliatory move in response to my refusal of delivery of the registered letter. It has always seemed to me cruelly disproportionate, but I am sure that the participants in the Near East conflict feel that way about each other's moves. My parents may have felt that I was harder to deal with than I realized.

That summer, I wanted to repair the motorcycle engine. I got it into my head to modify the engine to a fancy design I had seen in one of my books. This was a very ambitious undertaking, particularly for someone who did not yet understand the design principles. Dad tried to tell me that it probably would not work, at least in the time I had available, and that the motorcycle would then be without an engine, but when he saw that I was adamant, he left me alone. Of course, another motivation was to stay out of the house for the summer, since I was still smarting from the sale of the Nash.

It was finished just before I had to leave to go back to school, and inevitably, it would not start.

When I got back to school, I found that the motorcycle frame had disappeared. I never discovered whether it had been removed by Buildings and Grounds as an unsightly addition to the Harvard landscape or had been stolen by someone. I made inquiries, but no one knew anything. Theft of a motorless cycle seemed unlikely. However, all year my ear was listening for the sound of the engine. On one of the first nice days in the spring I heard through the open window of our fourth-floor room a sound exactly like the Royal Enfield. I raced to the window to see a motorcycle of the right size go past, with an identical buddy seat covered in yellow deerskin on the back.

Chapter 5

Junior year

HALF A BLOCK OFF MASSACHUSETTS Avenue, on the same street that led to Eliot House, was Cronin's, the college bar where we gathered every evening at 10:00, a large room with six long rows of booths, and hard-bitten middle-aged waitresses from south Boston who were well past being of the slightest interest to undergraduates. This establishment had been started by big Jim Cronin, who still appeared from time to time, but was run during my time there by Jim, his son. Young Jim died an untimely death, and John Sr. took over after I left. When the Harvard–Yale game was played in Cambridge, Jim would bring in his 11 or so brothers-in-law from Southie, and they would stand imposingly in long white aprons to maintain some kind of order in the madhouse, half an inch deep in spilled beer and sawdust.

Directly across from Cronin's was a men's wear store. In this store was a sleazy individual slightly older than we, who had had some vague connection with the university. My suspicion is that he had flunked out of some program or other.

One evening at Cronin's, about halfway through the fall semester, one of our group who was friendly with the sleazy individual across the way announced that his friend was getting married, and during the extended honeymoon he would place his car, a postwar MG, in the care of someone who could take care of it, but more importantly, someone who had a lockable garage in which to hide it, since he owed money on it and the repo men were looking for it.

I immediately began to inquire about lockable garages in Cambridge. Ones accessible by me were scarcer than hen's teeth; undergraduates whose families actually lived in Cambridge were extremely rare, and those with an unoccupied garage rarer still. However, I found one, and my friend agreed to let me park the MG in his garage for the duration of the honeymoon, which would be perhaps two months long.

At the time agreed upon, the sleazy individual turned over the keys with an ominous warning that there would be hell to pay if the car was repossessed under my care. I also agreed to maintain it, doing whatever was necessary to keep it in good health. The sleazy individual took off for Bermuda with his new bride.

I was ecstatic. The car was lovely. It ran, as a matter of fact, very poorly. The weather was getting bad, and it was difficult to find a place to work on it. Through a friend of a friend, we got access late at night to a well lit and relatively warm parking garage, where I sorted out one of the problems.

A little later, I got access to a lathe in one of the garages on Harvard Square, and rebuilt the generator. It still amazes me that they let me in to use their lathe. People are (or were) nicer to students than they are to adults.

By this time, I had a girl friend, who later became my wife. She was a Radcliffe student. When I had the MG, we used to take little trips for lunch out to a restaurant on Fresh Pond, which had a wonderful lobster stew, or down to South Station, which made an excellent oyster stew. We went parking in the MG, on the street next to her dorm.

Her family lived in Highland Park, New Jersey, a suburb of New Brunswick, where her father was chair of the English department at Rutgers. I had gone home with her several times before we had the MG, but now we decided to drive down.

We had had a couple of flat tires in the MG, and had discovered that Model A tires fitted, and were available from the junkyard off Central Square. I bought a gift selection of tires with reasonable tread, had them installed on the spare wheels, and we took off for Highland Park. It was winter, and the heater in the MG did not work. We got carried away, and since we were already so cold, we decided to put the top down and enjoy ourselves. Despite our initial belief, it was possible to be even colder with the top down, but we left it that way to enjoy the looks from passing motorists. Down and back we had a total of four flat tires, some of which involved separation of the tread from the carcass. These were tires of indeterminate age that had been in the junkyard for a long time. The jack that came with the MG was very unsatisfactory, and the car rolled on an uneven berm, which they all were. However, we got down to New Brunswick. In preparation for the trip back, we were outfitted with enough old clothes so that we could put on three pairs of pants each, and several sweaters. The primary effect of the extra clothing was to make it difficult to get behind the wheel. We were a little warmer on the way back, but again we put the top down.

Returning to Cambridge, Jane checked into the Radcliffe Health Center, where they treated her for pneumonia.

The MG honeymoon was coming to an end. Jane was at home recuperating. I had been out late drinking. I was awakened with a stunning hangover at what seemed the crack of dawn (but was probably 10:00) by the sleazy individual demanding his car.

After the first couple of nights, I had found that the locked garage in Cambridge was a good hike from Eliot House, and it was too much trouble, so I had been parking the MG on the streets around the Harvard houses. Since parking was extremely tight, the MG ended up in quite different locations each night, and I felt it was probably safe. I soon forgot about the deal about the garage.

When the sleazy individual showed up, I was too fuzzy-headed to lie convincingly, and it was soon clear that the car was on the street. He was livid. Then it became clear that I could not remember just where I had parked it. He was enraged. I tried to calm him with stories of the improvements I had made to the running of the car. He was not having any. I was to get dressed, locate the car immediately, and bring it to him forthwith. Actually, I did not have much trouble finding the car. I did not tell the sleazy individual, but I had been too far gone to drive home, and I had let a friend put the car to bed. Fortunately, he remembered where he had put it. I returned it, and I never saw it or the sleazy individual again.

With the beginning of this year I had found that my excellent training in high school had stretched as far as it was going to. If I were to stay in Harvard, I would have to start working. Also, my life had been stabilized by Jane. For the most part, I was getting up in time to go to class, and doing the homework. It is amazing how much easier a course is if you actually go to the lectures and read the book in a timely manner. (I had been getting by in the first two years by reading the book the night before the final exam.) However, this meant that the time available for cars was limited.

When Jane and I were in Highland Park one weekend, we went in to New York City for the evening. We had plans to have dinner in a small French restaurant, and wanted to visit the Metropolitan and the Museum of Modern Art in the afternoon. In between the museums and the dinner, we passed by J.S. Inskip, the largest Rolls-Royce and Bentley agent in the country. We were all dressed up for the evening, and we decided to go in. I had a wonderful time looking at the Rolls and Bentleys. (Since this was the spring of 1951, the Bentley would have been a Mk. VI, and the Rolls a

Silver Wraith. As I write this, I am restoring a Mk. VI Bentley, quite coin-cidentally.) I could not resist lying down on the floor so that I could slide under the car. Immediately a disapproving individual, in demeanor some-where between a butler and an undertaker, came over to ask my protrud-ing feet if he could help me. I think it had probably been some time since anyone had gotten under one of their cars. In fact, he was very friendly, and allowed us a brief tour of their shops.

In Cambridge, interesting cars used to appear from time to time. Some of the wonderful old houses on the North Shore had stunning cars in their extensive garages, and these might be brought out for a trip to Harvard on a nice spring day, say for senior week just before graduation. One year a beautiful Packard touring car appeared, with drum-shaped spotlamps mounted on pedestals at the front of the running boards. On another occasion a very fancy prewar Rolls *coupé de ville* showed up with repoussé basketweave door panels in what appeared to be German silver. I remember seeing a very nice Alvis, and another prewar Rolls, a limo with jump seats and a division. I often looked under these cars, or swung out from a parking meter to get a good look at the radiator, only to look up to find the owner looking back at me with bemusement.

I went home for the summer, and this year my parents had a deal for me. They needed a flagstone walk from the front door to the parking area, ending in flagstone steps down to the parking surface.

In exchange, I would get the car they had bought just after the war, a 1947 maroon Chevy. At only four years of age this was a young car, from any point of view, and I jumped at the chance.

Building the walk was a nightmare, since I knew nothing about trim-ming flagstones. I did not mind spending the summer crouched in the sun, but I wanted to do a nice job, and it was extremely frustrating to find it so difficult. I never did find the proper method of trimming the flags, so it took me much longer than it should have. In the end, however, the walk looked very nice, and I had a car of my own.

Chapter 6

Senior year

KEEPING A CAR IN CAMBRIDGE has both an up side and a down side. The upside is that on a nice day in spring you can take a bunch of friends to Nantasket beach on the spur of the moment, and savor the salt air and drink some beer. Or, you and your buddies can make a late-night trip to the Nile restaurant for some Egyptian food. Or, you can go out to Fresh Pond and savor the lobster stew again, or, if overcome with homesickness, you can drive down to Highland Park for a weekend.

The down side of having a car is parking. The university provides parking across the river, behind Soldiers' Field. That is a long walk, especially late at night. Trying to park in Cambridge during daylight hours, during the week, is a nightmare. I did it. It didn't make sense, but it meant that the car could be used from time to time on a whim, whereas when parked across the river, it was only usable with a lot of forethought. I would cruise the streets around the Harvard houses looking for a parking space. Of course, there were none. This is like looking for a parking space in New York City. What there were, however, were just a few spaces that were a little short. Perhaps a foot short. These were left as they were, since no one could fit into them. I would pick the largest, and enlarge it. Delicately snuggling my rear bumper up against the front bumper of the car behind, I would apply power and push it (against its set parking brake) back until its rear bumper was touching that of the car behind. Then, I would do the same for the car in front. This usually created enough extra length to shoehorn my car into the space. I did this for the better part of a year, and never had a nasty note under my wiper blade, or a ticket for this technique.

I did get tickets. Many of the parking spots I made were in illegal areas, and I would come back to find all the cars there ticketed. I am afraid I accumulated the tickets in the glove compartment of the car. By the end of the year, I had a fine collection of both Harvard University and City of Cambridge tickets. At one point in the late spring I began to worry that the existence of these unresolved tickets (at least the Harvard ones) might interfere with my graduation. I took the Harvard tickets into the Harvard University police office and was confronted by a large south Boston Irish cop of the old school. I told him that I had been sick, and during that time I had loaned my car to a friend. When I returned, I had been horrified to find in the glove compartment this collection of tickets. Of course, honor forbade me to divulge the name of my friend. God bless the cop, he let me get away with it. I can't believe he didn't suspect something, after a lifetime of being told tall tales by Harvard undergraduates. He didn't even tell me (as he might well have done) that since it was my car, I was responsible, and should make whatever arrangement I could to obtain reimbursement from my friend. I walked out scot-free. I could not possibly have paid them, and would have had to appeal to my parents, who would have taken it out of my hide.

Now it was time for the City of Cambridge. This was considerably more serious. These also amounted to what was a substantial sum for me then, several hundred dollars. Toward the end of the spring, I spent several days in the infirmary for something that seemed at first like appendicitis, but which went away by itself, and was probably nothing more than accumulated fatigue. While I was in there, I talked Jane into taking the tickets in to the City of Cambridge police headquarters to see what she could do. She actually did it, which was far more than I deserved. The south Boston Irish cop on the front desk was also fatherly. From watching years of cop shows on television, I understand now that they put the men who are close to retirement on the front desk, out of harm's way where their feet won't hurt. In any event, it worked out well for us. Jane told him about her brilliant fiancé who was sadly confined to the infirmary with something unidentified. She had found these tickets in the glove compartment of his car. Was there any way that she could take care of them? She could certainly not afford to pay them, but perhaps some arrangement could be made? I have to imagine all this on the basis of Jane's reports, since I was not there, but I understand that he was patting her hand by the time it was over, and reassuring her that she (and I) need not worry about anything.

After this, we did park the car across the river, and were assiduous about avoiding any new tickets, but we only had to manage this for a few weeks more.

The men in Jane's family had gone to graduate school and gotten doctorates. This was a possibility that had not occurred to me, but Jane was pushing for it, and it sounded attractive. When I mentioned it to my parents, suggesting perhaps becoming a professor, it got a mixed reaction. My father pointed out that he hired professors to show up at meetings with the clients to make an impression, and that most of the professors, in his experience, didn't have the sense to come in out of the rain. Mom said essentially that she hoped I didn't imagine that my family would pay for this escapade. And, didn't I think it was time to earn some money?

I went ahead anyway. I had not covered myself with glory academically, and was lucky to get admitted anywhere. At least partly on the basis of my modification of the motorcycle engine, I was admitted to Johns Hopkins. I was admitted provisionally, without financial support, my continued presence being contingent on my grades. I was ecstatic.

With Mom's agreement to provide partial support for one semester, I was home free (in a manner of speaking).

Meanwhile, my final Harvard semester drew to a close. Senior week is always heartbreakingly lovely. The weather is beautiful, and all the Houses have parties for their graduates. Striped tents are everywhere. Beautiful young women also. This is when the wonderful old cars make their annual appearance from the garages on the North Shore. Cynically, the whole show is probably concocted to leave an indelible impression, so that the new alumni will feel warmly disposed toward the alma mater. It works. It took decades of employment in academia before I was immunized.

I spent the summer working for Curtiss-Wright in Woodridge, New Jersey, and living with Jane's parents just outside New Brunswick. Every day I gritted my teeth against the Secaucus and Bayone smells, dodged 18-wheelers and listened to WQXR.

Just at the end of the summer, the car needed attention. All the pushing and shoving involved in creating longer parking spaces had worn out the clutch, and the engine needed rings and bearing shells. I did this in the garage of Jane's parents over a weekend. I am afraid it was a shock to their systems, although I tried to be as neat and clean as possible under the circumstances. They were nevertheless very gracious about it, and I went off to Baltimore with the car in good shape.

Chapter 7

Baltimore

LIFE WITHOUT JANE (who was finishing her last year at Radcliffe) was not much fun. We had long, inarticulate telephone calls, but they were a poor substitute. I decided to visit her in Cambridge, and did this every few weeks. I had a late class Friday afternoon, the timing arranged for the convenience of the students who worked for Bethlehem Steel Shipyards. The class was Elasticity, as I recall. It got out at 5:30. I would climb in my car and take off for Cambridge, picking up a hamburger on the road. Bear in mind that this was long before the construction of interstate highways. We are talking about US 1, the Pulaski Skyway, the Sawmill River Parkway, the Takonic State Parkway, and so on, ending up on Route 9 through Newton and Framingham. It was a very long drive.

On one of my visits to Jane's parents' house, I had expressed an interest in classical Greek. Jane's father had, as a professor of English literature, been required to have a certain fluency in Latin and Greek, as well as Old English, and he loaned me a beginning grammar of classical Greek. On the long drive to Boston, at a convenient traffic light, I would scan a declension, and then repeat it to myself as I drove along until it was burned into my memory. Then I would do another. It helped to keep me awake.

There was often fog on the Connecticut stretch, as the people who live there know all too well. Once, I was picked up for speeding at 2:00 in the morning by a Connecticut cop, and hauled in for summary justice. Bail was set, and a court date established. I did not have the money to pay my bail, and thought I might have to spend some time in jail, a new experience. However, the arresting officer was clearly sympathetic, and asked me if I had an AAA card. I did, as a matter of fact, courtesy of my parents. He pointed out that this card guaranteed bail (something contained in the fine print that I had never read), so, to my joy and disbelief, I was off the hook. As I left the station, the trooper said to me sotto voce, "Jeeze, I had all my lights on, didn't you see me?" Of course, I had been on automatic pilot by that time, and would probably not have noticed naked people cavorting on the berm.

Another time, as I came over a hill on a three-lane stretch of road just over the Massachusetts border, two 18-wheelers came over the crest toward me, neck-and-neck. I was blinded by fatigue and this sudden blaze from four headlights on high beam, and became completely disoriented; I slewed across the road, coming to rest on the opposite side in a sand bed, about three feet from a telephone pole. On the way across the road, I was aware of passing between the two trucks and one that had been following them. I was lucky to be alive, and proceeded with a little more caution, although what I mostly needed was sleep.

The trip back to Baltimore was anticlimactic, to say the least. Although just as long, it certainly seemed longer. I also left later, because I wanted to spend every possible minute with Jane. One morning about 3:00, my engine died abruptly somewhere in southern New Jersey. I knew immediately what had happened, because there was an overwhelming smell of acrylic. The laminated fabric timing gear had stripped. A passing cop called for a tow truck from an all-night garage, and I arranged for them to fix it in the next few days, while I caught a bus to Baltimore. I was infinitely suspicious, but in fact they did a very nice job at a reasonable price.

Somehow I got through the year and did not get killed on the highway. Spring came to Baltimore, with profusions of azaleas in Greenwood Gardens, and tulip trees on the campus.

Jane taught school, for which Radcliffe had not prepared her, trying to cope with second grade juvenile delinquents.

Jane drove the car back and forth to work. I would get occasional frantic calls because the car would not behave. In effect, it was a one-person car — it always behaved for me, and constantly let Jane down. When I arrived to answer an emergency call, it would usually behave perfectly. The only thing I could not fix was the column gearshift. It was what we used to call "three on the tree." Column shifts were very popular with the car companies at that time, but gradually passed out of existence. Ours had a very worn linkage, which required long division to tell what gear you were in.

At about this time, my parents bought one of the slightly used cars from the GM executive just up the street. This meant they had a car to

The Mercury, photographed at my parents' house in Birmingham, Michigan. Mom is next to it, and her garden is in the background. She thought that coat was terribly elegant.

spare, and they gave it to us. It was a 1949 Mercury woody station wagon in a pale yellow called Bermuda Cream. Although it was nearly the same age as the Chevy it had far fewer miles and had been maintained very carefully. It was lovely. Jane and I went over to Washington to collect it. Mom was a delegate to the Republican National Convention that year, so this must have been 1955. She and Dad had driven east for the convention, and had brought the station wagon. We were delighted to have it.

By this time we had two kids and needed a station wagon to transport the enormous amount of stuff required. Whenever we went up to Highland Park to visit Jane's parents, cribs, highchairs, bassinets, diaper pails and so forth were folded and stacked and packed into the back of the station wagon. Driving out to Detroit to see my parents, we felt that we could not stop at a motel — we could not afford it, to begin with — so, we slept in the car in shifts. We put a small mattress in the back of the station wagon, and drove all night. To make room for this the paraphernalia had to go on top, and I designed and fabricated a monster roof rack. On the first trip to Detroit with this equipment, the return trip was threatened by rain, and Dad sprang for a tarpaulin to fit the gigantic rack.

I finally got my degree in 1957. It had been delayed for a year, while I dithered over whether my thesis was worthy or not. I stayed on as a postdoc for a couple of years, while we had our third child, Chris.

Chapter 8

Penn State

I GOT MY FIRST JOB at Penn State. Our things were professionally moved to State College (the town in which Penn State's home campus is located) into a real house on a street lined with elm trees just a few blocks from campus. When we moved, the kids were five, four and one, so Jane was occupied full time taking care of them.

After a couple of years there, the Mercury was looking pretty tired. A woody wagon has to be cared for like a wooden boat and refinished every year or two. Of course, I never did anything to it, and the wood had been without much finish for some time, had rotted, and had acquired ear-type fungi of the type seen on rotting logs in the forest. It was very sad, because it had been a pretty car, and a reliable one. The Ford flat-head V8 is an indestructible engine, and it never gave us any trouble. It did have a carburetor float valve that tended to stick from time to time, but we had carried a rubber mallet under the front seat since the car was young; one sharp blow to the carburetor bowl was usually enough.

The Mercury had also had a transmission problem at the end: reverse gear had ceased to exist, and we could not afford to have it fixed. We learned to seek out parking spaces that were either uphill or level. In the uphill ones, we simply drifted out backwards. In the level ones, presuming there was a curb, we learned to bounce the front tires against the curb, which gave us just enough momentum backward to get out of the space. We managed for the better part of a year this way. But, it was definitely time for it to go.

We were quite taken with the VW bus, which was just sweeping the country. This was about 1961. We bought a green one, with the original 25 HP engine. For our trips out to Detroit to see my parents, I arranged plywood planks supported by the backs of the seats, and we bedded the kids down on the floor. We usually camped near Vermillion, Ohio, on the lake. All this was not too satisfactory, because the kids, who were still quite young, did not enjoy this camping experience much and did not go to sleep. The adults did not find the plywood planks particularly comfortable either, and were quite cranky when they were kept up by the kids.

At work, I got a number of comments about our choice of vehicle; my colleagues thought it was pretty funny that we had gone from a station wagon with mushrooms to the most underpowered vehicle on the road. After a couple of years of this, we went looking again. We were actually quite happy with the bus design, but we saw a red camper and fell in love.

I had been invited to spend six weeks at Stanford in the summer. We had just built a house in a new development, and had planted a new lawn in the treeless expanse that had been a farmer's field a couple of years before. We left a friend with the responsibility of watering the nascent lawn, and took off for Palo Alto in the camper, with Vonnie, a friend from Baltimore who would play the role of baby sitter.

We camped across the country. Jane and I slept on the pullout bed, the kids slept on the seats in the tiny breakfast nook, and on the floor between the seats, and Vonnie slept on the front seat. This arrangement was fine for about three hours. During this time, the exhalations of six people gradually raised the humidity inside the bus until the atmosphere resembled an equatorial rainforest. At this point I often got up and moved outside, putting up a cot and getting into my sleeping bag.

We stayed one night at Cahokia Mounds, just across the river from St. Louis. These Indian mounds were fascinating, but we were in danger of being carried off by the largest and most numerous mosquitoes that I had ever seen. We also stopped in South Dakota for dinner, at a roadside picnic table. As soon as we got out of the bus, swarms of huge mosquitoes decided that we were dinner, and with one mind we turned and ran for the bus, swatting as we went. We ate dinner huddled inside, trying to kill the ones that had gotten in with us.

Going across Kansas, the wind blew ceaselessly from the prairies of Canada. The bus had the aerodynamics of a billboard, and I had to struggle with the wheel to keep it headed straight. After a couple of days of this, I became convinced that there was something the matter with the front suspension. In Hayes, Kansas, we stopped and visited a VW agency, which undertook to check the front end alignment while we visited a local museum. We were bemused by the museum, which displayed artifacts from 1860, such as a parlor organ, as though they were rare and obscure objects. From Jane's family, we had inherited a number of things of similar and much greater age, with which we lived on a daily basis. For example, we also had a parlor organ, as well as an eighteenth century desk. In the end, the agency said there was nothing the matter with the front alignment; it was just the wind.

We made it to Palo Alto, but the engine was in trouble. We took the bus to a local agency, and they sadly told us that it needed a full rebuild. This seemed unlikely to me, considering the mileage, but I had never worked on one of these, and we had certainly driven it hard. It had been running essentially flat out since we left State College. So, I had a rebuilt engine dropped in.

On the way back, just east of Needles, we spent the night at the side of the road. As usual, in the middle of the night I couldn't stand the humidity, and set up a cot outside the door. In the morning a state trooper came by as we were having breakfast. He was very cordial and courteous, and said that he had been by during the night and had checked to make sure that my arms were inside my sleeping bag. I looked at him quizzically. "Well, you see," he explained, "the rattlers like to come up to the road when the sun goes down, because the road is warm, and if your arm is out of the sleeping bag, trailing on the ground, they will crawl up the arm to get into the nice warm bag with you." I have never felt quite the same about camping since then.

As soon as we got back I cut a hole in the roof of the bus and put in a large vent. We did go camping again a few times after this, and it was a big improvement. However, we more or less decided that we were not camping types.

Patty got married in Baltimore, and we all went down to the wedding. We were trying to make time the way we usually did, by flooring the bus on the way down each hill, so that we would have enough momentum to get up the next one. Remember, we only had 25 horsepower. Somewhere around Timonium, the engine ground to a halt. We had the bus towed to the nearest VW garage, rented a car and proceeded to the wedding. Although this cast an initial pall over the trip, we ultimately had a lovely time.

Coming back, we stopped at the VW agency to see our bus. They had the engine apart and showed us the interior. There were neat holes in all the piston crowns, and the inside of the engine was splattered with gobs of molten aluminum. Going flat out down the hills was overspeeding the engine, allowing the piston crown temperature to get above the melting point. We had them put in a rebuilt engine, and I came back for the bus a few days later. These educational experiences were getting expensive.

Since we now lived in a suburb that was certainly not within walking distance of the campus, it was extremely awkward having only one car. We scraped together a little money and bought a used Saab. This was a three cylinder, two stroke cycle engine. It was essential to remember to put oil in the gasoline. When we first got the Saab, the left rear shock was not attached (the attachment point on the body had rusted away), and under power it would produce a truly startling hopping. However, I had that welded, and it was fine. One day, Jane took several little old ladies out to lunch in the Saab. On the way back, they had some engine trouble and called on our local gas station. The pump jockey came out in the tow truck, popped open the hood, and stood there scratching his head, finally saying that he "ain't never seen nothing like that afore."

I am sorry to say that someone forgot, twice, to put oil in the gas, and cooked the engine. I would not consider trying to assign blame. By the time the engine was cooked, the responsible event was usually several days in the past, so that no one could remember the details. Fortunately, these engines were quite popular for racing and were very simple, so they were available and relatively inexpensive.

It was 1966, and time for my first sabbatical. The kids were now roughly eight, ten and twelve. We had decided to spend most of this year in Marseilles, France, at the turbulence institute there, with shorter stays in Grenoble and in Cambridge. Jane's father had died unexpectedly a few years before, and her mother now lived in State College. We decided to take her with us on sabbatical. Jane also wanted to take our two golden retrievers.

At that time it was still possible to get a very good deal on a foreign car, taking delivery at the factory and bringing it back with you. Jane's mother very generously offered to pay for a Citroën ID 21 station wagon. I was ecstatic. In addition, I had enough spare cash to arrange for a Triumph Spitfire, which would be delivered directly to New York at the end of the year, but the price of which would benefit from our temporary presence in England.

We sold the bus and the Saab, and left for New York. I had to fly to a meeting in Tokyo, and would catch up with the family in Paris. Everybody else would take the France to Le Havre.

When the meeting in Tokyo was finished, I caught a plane for Paris. These were the days when the Soviet Union did not permit overflights, so that a flight from Tokyo to Paris went via Hong Kong, Bangkok, Bombay, Karachi, Teheran, Cairo, and Rome, and took 24 hours. At every airport we were required to leave the plane and wait in the airport lounge while the plane was fumigated. Sleep was virtually impossible. I was not in very good condition on arrival in Paris.

After a day or so, the kids and I went out to the Citroën plant in a suburb of Paris to collect our car. The car was magnificent. This Citroën in particular was of a very felicitous design, very elegant. The only one better looking, to my eye, was the Citroën-Maseratti, which was similar. There is nothing quite like a brand new car, in any case — the upholstery, the carpeting, the paint, the smell. And, it is so perfect, so without a flaw. It is easy to understand the Arab idea that perfection attracts the evil eye. I started to feel uneasy about the prospect of getting this perfect thing back to the hotel. We headed back to Paris, and everything was fine. However, it was the evening rush hour. As we approached Paris, the traffic thickened. When it seemed that it could not get any thicker, it did. This was my first experience of French traffic, which I eventually learned to negotiate with the best of the taxi drivers. Now, however, I was fresh from the States, and driving a

The only picture we have of the Citroën, and not much of it at that. Photographed in our driveway in Marseilles. One of the kids' friends (looking at camera) and Jennifer.

brand new car. We had to pass through the Place de l'Etoile just at 5:30, possibly the worst time of day, in the most congested intersection, in the city with the worst traffic, in what is probably the second worst country in the world as far as traffic problems are concerned. I understand that Thailand is worse, although I have never driven there. Space is at such a premium in French cities that French drivers have come to regard an inch or two as a reasonable clearance. I was having a cow. We actually got back to the hotel without a scrape, but I think I was ten years older.

The next day, with the help of a bellhop, we packed the car for the trip to Marseilles. Everything went on top. There was a full roof-rack, and with the suitcases standing up, the roof of the car was completely covered to a depth of two feet. All this was covered with a tarpaulin. Jane's mother and the kids occupied the second seat and the two jump seats in the way-back, along with the dogs.

The Citroën had a semiactive suspension, which adjusted automatically for height. The car could be loaded as much as you wished, and the suspension would compensate, maintaining the set height. Eventually, if this process was carried too far, you would blow out the seals in the hydraulic system, which we did, just before leaving France. For now, however, the load on the roof seemed just fine. As the suspension adjusted to the increased load, the pneumatic springs got stiffer, so that the ride remained the same. A similar thing happened with the aerodynamic loading: as the speed went up, and the load increased on the front (due to the sloping hood) the spring stiffness increased also, but now (since this was due to aerodynamic load, and not mass) this had the effect of making the suspension more rigid, so that the car felt as though it were on rails. We drove the car at 80 mph all day long, and it was wonderful.

At one point, we went in for a long French lunch, leaving the dogs in the car. When we came out, we found that they had become a little bored, and had eaten the inch-thick foam rubber padding under the front carpet. Scraps were strewn everywhere in our beautiful car. Fortunately, when we had cleaned up the scraps, and put the carpet back where it belonged (the carpet itself was not damaged), the damage was almost invisible. We learned to live with it.

We drove the Citroën everywhere that year. We hunted for a house or apartment in it, threading our way through tiny alleys, with the kids hanging out the back windows telling me what the clearance was. I argued with taxis until I understood *priorité au droite*. I waited for Jane outside a store in the Arab *quartier* (the only one open on a Christian holiday) so she could buy a forgotten sack of coal to heat the house (the Arabs could not have been more courteous). We took the kids skiing at Gap in it.

The car had a recurrent problem that had become apparent within a day of our picking it up. At high speed it ran fine, but at the speeds of French traffic the spark plug in the number four cylinder gradually loaded up and began to miss. When removed, it was oil fouled. I took it in to several agencies to talk to them about it, but my French was not persuasive, and they gave me the runaround. They did not want to get involved with a foreigner with a problem (who, after all, would be expected to disappear conveniently after a certain delay). This problem continued as long as we owned the car. After we got home, the plug was in and out so many times that the threads were stripped, and I had to put in a Helicoil insert. I am convinced now that that cylinder had a broken ring.

Just before Christmas in Marseilles, we were about to leave for Turin to visit some friends from State College who were also on sabbatical. We were doing a hundred things to get ready to leave, dashing madly about. I went on a last-minute errand to get something that I have now forgotten. I jumped in the car and took off. Our street took a single-lane dogleg before entering the extension of the Corniche along the ocean front. Intent on my errand, I entered this without honking, only to encounter a taxi on its way in. It was raining lightly, and there was almost no traction. Both cars were put out of action. We exchanged insurance cards and called for the tow truck. He was very polite, especially considering that I had put him out of business. The accident had taken place right in front of the mom-and-pop store where we got our bread and milk, and the proprietor and the patrons came out to enjoy the spectacle. It was the talk of the *quartier* for days. I felt terribly guilty, because it was certainly my fault, but also heartbroken because I had destroyed the beautiful car, far more opulent than anything that we had ever had before.

Of course, we had to make other arrangements to go to Turin. I rented a Peugeot 404, and we left, in a dismal mood. On the hairpin turns mounting to the alpine pass, as the car swayed from side to side, Jenny threw up out the window regularly.

After we arrived in Turin, our mood gradually improved as we basked in the gracious hospitality of our friends. In addition to excellent meals, they gave us a royal tour of Turin, including the automobile museum.

By the time we got back from Turin, the very professional Citroën agency had returned the car to its pristine state. Amazing! In order to register the car in France, we had had to obtain very expensive insurance, with full collision coverage. I had resented the enormous cost, but now it paid off, because the insurance company reimbursed the costs without a murmur.

Toward the end of our year in Europe, we spent a couple of months in Cambridge. We had parked the dogs in a kennel in France and sent the kids to live with my parents in Devon. Chris was enrolled in the local public school, but the girls were country day students at a nearby private girls' school that had primarily boarders.

When Dad had retired, my parents had returned to an England they had not seen for 50 years. All that time in the States they had held themselves apart from the culture surrounding them, regarding it with disapproval, and feeling themselves to be British (Mom was Scottish), although they had made successful, Herculean efforts to rid themselves of the least trace of accent (resulting in speech patterns far too correct for local ears). It was poetic justice that the English now considered them Americans.

Several times we drove down from Cambridge to visit the kids and my parents in Devon. I had often rented cars on my trips to England, so I was accustomed to driving on the left. However, the rented cars had of course had right-hand drives. Now we were driving the left-hand-drive Citroën on the highways in Devon. This is when you discover whether your marriage is really sound. Seated in the left seat, the driver cannot possibly see whether it is safe to pass. The wife, in the right seat, watches for a passing opportunity, and shouts "Go!" The driver must pull out immediately, with total trust, unable to see anything until it is too late.

When we returned from England, we spent an uneventful month in Grenoble at another turbulence laboratory, and then passed a couple of weeks driving up the Rhine valley to Copenhagen, where we spent a few days with friends. We then descended via Cologne and Reims to Le Havre, where we were to take the *France*. The drive up the Rhine valley was beautiful but frightening. We were on the autobahn, constructed just before the Second World War by Hitler to facilitate troop movements. It was not designed for modern speeds, and was intended to carry far less traffic than it carries at present. There is no speed limit. The traffic density is similar to the Los Angeles freeways, but the cruising speed is between 80 and 90 mph. You have to keep up with the traffic flow. Every few minutes, the driver sees headlights in the rear view mirror, flashing up and down, far back but coming up fast. This is a signal to get out of the passing lane. In a moment you will be able to identify a very large Mercedes, moving at perhaps 120–150 mph, bulldozing everything out of the way. In an instant, it is gone, vanishing into the distance, as the traffic cringes to the right to keep out of its way. Once or twice a day you will see on the berm the remains of an accident, sometimes with the victims still sitting holding their heads and waiting for the ambulance. The kids in the back were terrified, and so was I. Since then, I have spent a lot of time driving on the highways of France, Italy and Germany, but this drive was by far the most frightening.

The day we arrived in Le Havre, we blew out the seals in the hydraulic system (specifically in the steering rack), presumably due to carrying too much luggage. We were a day early, and had 24 hours before we were to board the boat. I did not believe that we could have the car repaired in State College (and, boy, was I right), so Christopher and I took it down to the local Citroën agency and begged and pleaded with them. They actually made the repair in the time available, God bless them, and we boarded the boat the next day without incident.

When we got back to State College, the Citroën served us faithfully for several years. It continued to be a wonderful car to drive. Then it began to have the normal problems of a middle-aged car. One of the hydraulic hoses came adrift. It began to have starter problems. There was a Citroën agency in town, but they seemed to have difficulty getting parts. I finally figured out that they were going bankrupt and nobody would extend them credit. They could only get parts if they were willing to pay cash in advance, and they couldn't do that because they had no cash. In a couple of cases I advanced them the cash so they could send for the part, but eventually the inevitable happened, and they closed their doors. I think ours was nearly the only Citroën in town, so it was hardly surprising.

With great sadness, we decided to sell the car. This was a stupid decision. It was the best car we have ever owned, in terms of overall drivability. I could have maintained it, if I had decided to make the necessary effort. I did not have enclosed space to work on a car, but that had never stopped me before. Certainly, since that time, I have gotten involved with the restoration of rare cars, and have had to obtain parts from around the world; parts for the Citroën could not have been any more difficult to get. In any event, we advertised it, and immediately got a buyer who flew in from New Jersey to look at it. He liked it and agreed to buy it. He would come back to collect it in a couple of weeks.

Katy was just learning to drive, just about to get her license. The new station wagon that would replace the Citroën was parked on the road in front of the house, behind the Citroën, and needed to be moved into the driveway. Katy begged to be allowed to do this. We thought she could handle it, and thought it would be good for her self-confidence. We were still at the dinner table, and she went out to move the car. A moment later there was a crash. We all rushed out to see what had happened. Katy had somehow driven the new station wagon into the back of the Citroën. The new car was not significantly damaged, but the Citroën tailgate was crushed.

Fortunately, there was an exceptional body shop in town, which did hammer and dolly work and did not use filler. They later went out of business because people were not willing to pay their prices, but they did a splendid job on the Citroën. The buyer collected his car, perfectly satisfied with the condition (he had been a little apprehensive when I told him about the accident). We have missed it ever since.

Late in the fall of the year we returned from sabbatical, the Spitfire was finally delivered to New York, and I went down to collect it. There had been interminable shipping delays. The car had come by what is called RO-RO; Roll On, Roll Off. That is, it was driven onto a boat together with a thousand others, strapped down, and transported. I found the prospect of collecting this car terribly exciting; I had always wanted a sports car. When I arrived at the dock warehouse to collect the car, it was dark, and the place was empty except for me and the people I was dealing with, who might have been members of Tony Soprano's family. It was apparent that the car had been damaged in shipment, and repaired. The hood did not quite fit correctly. They admitted that the car had been badly (their word) damaged, and gave me a look that defied me to make something of it. I am afraid I was craven, and accepted delivery of the car as it was. Besides, I couldn't bear to not drive it home, the probable alternative. Also, I could envision more interminable delays while something was or was not done to improve the condition, and ultimate delivery of the car in an imperceptibly changed condition. It was good enough. I could live with it.

I had a wonderful time driving it home; it really was a blast to drive. My kids thought so too. They would all soon have driving licenses, and as soon as they did, they begged to borrow the Spitfire. After one of these borrowings, I was driving in to work when another driver yelled to me that my wheel was falling off. I thought this was unlikely, but there was probably something wrong. I found that one of the rear axle shafts had been bent, causing the wheel to wobble. This was the first of many half-shafts I replaced. I finally made the connection, but I never did identify exactly what my kids were doing to the car to result in bending the half-shafts. I presume they were throwing it around corners at high speed, possibly slamming the rear end into curbs. Of course, everybody denied everything.

At about this time, Jennifer developed a love affair with a Jeep. Not a particular Jeep, but she desperately wanted a Jeep. In rural areas there were usually plenty of these available, which had been bought surplus from the government by men who had been in one war or another and who had retained a fondness for the vehicle. They were usually used for snow plowing or hunting. We found a Jeep that was acceptable to her. They are fairly indestructible, but they do eventually wear out. This one had a severe oil leak from the rear main seal, and virtually no compression. I put rings and bearing shells in it, a new head gasket, and three new rear main seals. Three, because I could not seem to get it right. The third time it worked. Jenny drove the Jeep happily for several years.

The girls had a continual stream of boyfriends. When I had had to insert a Helicoil in the number four spark plug hole of the Citroën, Katy's boyfriend at the time had offered me much free advice. He was a remarkably large and handsome young man who was painfully dumb. Jenny also had a boyfriend about this time. Jenny's boyfriend was considerably smarter. He was very interested in her, but she wasn't much interested in him. In any event, he was having car troubles. His clutch needed to be replaced, and he needed a place to do it. It was winter, and we only had a carport, the walls of which did not come down to the ground, but we offered our services. When I came home, I found him under his car, wrestling with the transmission; the car was supported on two scissor jacks, placed flush against each front wheel. I nearly had heart failure. I told him to get out from under the car, and not to get under again until I got back; that I would be back in a half hour. I went downtown and bought two solid jackstands. When I came back, I got under with him, and together we got the transmission out, replaced the clutch, and then tried to replace the transmission. We tried to soak up the spilled oil with sand, of which I had a plentiful supply for the driveway in winter, so you have to imagine us lying in the sand and oil, in winter, with the wind howling under the walls of the carport, supporting the transmission over our heads, trying to get the input shaft into the hole in the clutch plate, grunting at each other. Even though the clutch plate is put in with a dummy shaft to line it up, the input shaft of the transmission will almost never go easily into the hole, and it is essential not to let the transmission hang on the shaft, because various things can be bent. Transmissions are very heavy.

We spent our second sabbatical year, 1973–74, in Liège (Belgium), Lyons and Marseilles. I had to attend a meeting in the Soviet Union, and Chris and I flew to Moscow after seeing Jane and Jennifer off on the *Michelangelo*. (Katy was still at Antioch, but would come over in the summer.) When the meeting was over, Chris and I flew from Moscow to Milan, where we took the streetcar to the Fiat factory and picked up a brand new Fiat 128 station wagon. We then drove down to Genoa and picked up Jane and Jennifer. This drive was my first experience of Italian drivers on the autostrada, and I shocked Chris by making what I imagined were very Italian gestures at the drivers who did the more egregious things. In Genoa, we loaded the new roof-rack with all our luggage and drove to Belgium.

We spent the first semester of the sabbatical in Liège. Jennifer had enrolled in an art school there, the Institut St. Luc, to be with us for a while. Her boyfriend Tom (of transmission fame) came over for Christmas, and they broke up. When we descended to Marseilles and Lyons, she stayed in Liège. Katy and her boyfriend Robert (who would become her husband) came over for the summer and worked in a campground just outside Lyons. Katy waited on tables and Robert cleaned the toilets. They were terribly exploited, and hated it, but at least we got to see them from time to time.

At the end of the fall semester, we descended to Marseilles, where we stayed for a few months. I was working on the east side of town, off the road to Cassis, at Luminy, where a huge air-sea interaction tunnel had been built.

In the spring, we left and went up to Lyons. We were there in mid-summer, counting the days until we should start for home. I was crossing a square downtown when I stopped for a light and looked into the rear view mirror. To my horror, I saw a taxi behind me, and the driver was waving gaily to a friend on the sidewalk, and had not seen me. I braced for the collision. It was not terribly serious, but the tailgate and rear lights were smashed and inoperable. We could not go back to the States that way. The regional agency agreed to fix it on a rush basis, but then they discovered that some of the lighting parts were to U.S. specification and were unobtainable in Europe. They did a very neat job using parts from a Renault, and got it done just in time for us to leave.

When it came time to leave, we drove to Genoa to take the *Leonardo da Vinci*, the sister ship of the *Michelangelo*.

I always thought the Fiat was a charming car. After it got over its teething problems it behaved beautifully. It was reasonably cheap, reasonably roomy and reasonably fast — what more could one ask? Jane hated it. We kept it on our return until it fell apart from rust; then we had Chris weld it back together. Not long afterward, a pump jockey left the oil filler cap off, and the engine was fried. We got another engine from the junkyard, and I put rings and bearing shells in it before dropping it in. We finally bequeathed the car to Katy and her family, who used it for a couple of years more. Toward the end, the steering rack failed, and Robert drove home, stopping every few yards to get out and aim the front wheels by hand. He finally abandoned it in a field half a mile from the house. On our next trip down, I installed a rebuilt rack where the car sat in the field. It lasted a while longer, but eventually the rust damage was beyond repair.

Chapter 9

VW memories (mostly)

OUR FIRST VW BEETLE was bought from the Johnsons, who lived in the same development as we, just around the bend in the road. Mr. Johnson had died of liver cancer. The bug had been their second car. It was in beautiful, pristine condition, a lovely robin's egg blue, and we got it for a good price.

Jennifer had come home from the Institut St. Luc in Liège, Belgium, after '73–'74, and we talked her into going to a real full-service college, against all her instincts. She went off to Bennington in the fall of '74, with the blue Beetle.

Jenny hated Bennington. She felt that the art program was a fraud, and the rest of the place was a country club. We were enjoying having a daughter at Bennington. After all, we could stop at *Hemmings Motor News* on the way into town, and at the Bennington Pottery on the way home, and have a meal at a chichi restaurant while we were there. And, Bennington (both town and college) was photogenic. Sadly, in the spring of '75, she led us through the faculty art exhibit, and we all agreed that she should not continue. She headed back to the Institut St. Luc for the '75-'76 academic year and temporarily bequeathed her bug to Chris, who was at Putney.

Katy had had a two-door, 120 series Volvo, one of the ones that looks a little like a 1949 Ford, probably from the early '60s. It had very little compression, burned oil, and had either a weak battery or a bad starter or both. It cranked very unenthusiastically, but always started. It had slabs of Bondo on the sides, put there by a garage so that it would pass inspection. Pennsylvania requires that the body not have jagged, sharp areas (such as those caused by rust), so that if you hit a pedestrian, the body will not be mutilated.

In the spring of '75, Katy was to go to a wildlife refuge in British Columbia and participate in a project to radio-tag and track cougars. But, she had to get there. The Volvo was starting less and less willingly. She needed another car. We had had a good experience with Jenny's VW, and Beetles were plentiful and cheap. We searched the ads in the local paper.

We found a 1965 bug and went to see it. It seemed fine. The price was right. It was being sold by a man of the cloth, which gave me a certain unmerited confidence. When it came time to pay him, he suggested falsifying the bill of sale in order to defraud the state of its sales tax. His words were, "I feel I've paid enough sales tax this year, don't you?" He then made a cryptic comment about situational ethics. While I did not object in principle to this, I was a bit taken aback to have it suggested by a man of the cloth. I should have been suspicious. When we got the car home and took a really good look at the engine, we found that it was in terrible condition. This gave me an opportunity to rebuild a VW engine.

I discovered J.C. Whitney. This is a mail order house in Chicago that has cheap parts for cheap cars. They had many pages of parts for Beetles, most of them from Brazil or Scandinavia. It was wonderful — it was now possible to buy sets of cylinders and pistons to increase the displacement at an astonishingly reasonable price. Of course, this was made possible by the construction of the engine, which was air cooled and had separate cylinders. I happily sent away for everything needed to rebuild Katy's engine, upgrading it to 1200 cc. I included an external oil cooler. The factory oil cooler was reputed to block the air flow to the forward cylinder on the left side, resulting in that cylinder failing first under difficult circumstances.

I also discovered what is known as *The Idiot Book*. This is not its proper title, which is something like *Repairing and Maintaining Your VW for the Compleat Idiot*. This is possibly the best guide to repair of a specific make of automobile that has ever been written. The Beetle and the bus had become the transportation of choice for a generation of flower children, blissed out on pot and penniless. Most of them were not mechanical, or at least had had no training, and had no money to have their vehicles professionally repaired. They needed help. *The Idiot Book* provided exactly what was needed. In language that appealed to, and could be understood by, the intended audience, the author led them by the hand through every procedure necessary for the maintenance of these vehicles. VW actually puts out excellent shop manuals, but you need training to understand them. *The Idiot Book* requires no training, and it contains in addition a wealth of information invaluable to an owner and otherwise obtainable only by experience. Now the Internet provides a forum in which someone planning to carry out a complicated and unfamiliar procedure can obtain generous helpings of advice. The Internet did not exist in 1975, and *The Idiot Book* met that need. I was at first a little ashamed to admit that I used it, but it was invaluable. After all, an air cooled, rear-engined vehicle has lots of peculiarities, and *The Idiot Book* is a painless way to learn about them fast. One of the advantages of being human is that it is possible to learn from the mistakes of others; it is not always necessary to make your own.

I even ordered an engine jack, necessary to remove the rear engine from the chassis. It is necessary to remove the engine to do nearly anything of any significance to a Beetle engine. In some cases, it may not be absolutely necessary, but the mechanic will soon find that it is easier. Removing and replacing the engine in a Beetle is sort of like removing and replacing the transmission in a normal car, only more so. The transaxle (both transmission and differential) has the input shaft sticking out, like a normal transmission; the engine, which carries the clutch plate, is about what two men can carry if their backs are in good condition. You need a jack with a platform on which the engine can be balanced; the jack needs to be on wheels so that the teetering pile of jack plus engine can be moved back and forth and from side to side to line up the input shaft with the hole in the clutch plate. With a little practice, the engine can be removed or replaced in 15 minutes or so.

It was nice to be rebuilding an engine again. There is great peace to be found in the work. It is demanding; care and precision are important; but if the rules are followed meticulously you end up with something very satisfying that is esthetically pleasing and is almost alive. When I got it back in the car, it started right up and sounded wonderful.

I had had the cylinder heads (which is to say, the valves) reconditioned by a local machine shop. The engine sounded lovely, and we waved goodbye to Katy and her friends who were participating in the cougar tracking.

She got out to Vancouver and Antioch West, and had a fine time tracking cougars. On the way home, near Chicago, the engine died. We did not hear about this until Katy arrived home. When she pulled into the driveway, there was an engine wrapped in a blanket on the back seat. Katy had driven directly to the local junkyard and bought an engine, negotiating to have it installed on the spot. Then she wrapped the dead engine in a blanket and had it put on the back seat. She felt that since I had put so much work into it, she should bring it home to me to resuscitate.

I rebuilt the engine again, and traded it for the one from the junkyard.

Jennifer and Christopher with Katy's Beetle at Katy and Robert's house.

The shop that had done the head had gotten the valve guides a little tight and they had seized up under power.

I eventually replaced the heater channels in this car. The heater channels formed the edges of the floor well, bringing tepid cooling air from the engine into the passenger compartment. Typically, the inner fender well behind the front wheel rusted out, exposing the front end of the heater channel. The spinning wheel drove salty slush into the exposed channel, where it melted and ran back along the side of the car, rotting everything. Fortunately, the Danes fabricated sturdy replacement channels that could be welded in.

This car lasted for a number of years, until Katy was rear-ended on the Benner Pike, between State College and Bellefonte. It was replaced by a slightly newer Beetle with a melted plastic dashboard. A pack of matches had ignited in the ashtray, resulting in a reduced price. Katy and Robert eventually took this on their honeymoon in 1980, and called from Sudbury, Canada, when they encountered voltage regulator problems.

From the point of view of initial cost and reparability, a used Beetle was the ideal entry-level car for a young person, and they were ubiquitous. A young friend of the family, David, had an aging VW bug. He was very unmechanical, and did not take care of the car, which was not unusual.

In particular, he did not adjust the valves as the owner's manual suggests. We do not need to go into the details, but what happens then is that the valve head gets so hot that the valve neck fractures, and the head falls into the cylinder. There is no room for it there, and it breaks the top of the piston to make a little room. This is how most VW Beetle engines die. David's engine died this way on the interstate in the fall of '75, and he called us for help. Robert and Chris were dispatched to collect him in a snowstorm.

The cost of rebuilding the engine professionally was more than the value of the car, and in any event more than David could afford. David sold us the car for a nominal fee, in return for us picking it up from the berm of the interstate.

The blue Beetle would have to go back to Jenny when she returned at the end of the academic year, and Chris would be without a car. We agreed to give David's bug to Chris, if he would rebuild the engine. We pulled the engine, and sent it off with Chris to Putney in the back seat of the blue Beetle. He rebuilt it as a senior project, on the desk and bed in his dormitory room (Putney is an informal kind of place). He moved into the closet for the duration. When it came time to mount the flywheel, it required a torque greater than his torque wrench could provide. He weighed himself, calculated how long a piece of pipe he would have to stand on to produce the torque, and did it. At the end of the year he and his friends rappelled the engine down from the third floor dormitory window using their rock-climbing gear, and brought it home to State College in the back of our Fiat.

We installed the engine in David's bug, and tried to start it. As long as we were pouring gas down the carburetor, it would run beautifully, but as soon as we stopped, it did too. We could not sort it out for the moment, and Chris had a job at Elm Lea Farm (the Putney farm) and had to get back. In the fullness of time, I discovered a nest of insects in the fuel pump. When these were removed, the engine ran beautifully.

Jenny had taken back her blue Beetle, and we had sent Chris back to Elm Lea Farm with the Spitfire while I figured out what was the matter with his Beetle. While he had it, he practiced his gas welding skills (which he had learned in sculpture class) by making and installing rocker panels. Then he painted them. He did a beautiful job.

We traded cars again, and he took his Beetle up to Elm Lea Farm with him. During the winter of '76-'77, he was driving his friend Jonathan home from Putney when he began to have problems. By the time they had arrived at Jonathan's mother's house, the car was undrivable. A little exploration suggested that the flywheel had come loose. Chris now feels that he should have pulled the engine right there and fixed it himself. However, he called me, and I borrowed a Thunderbird from my next-door neighbor, rented a towing hitch and went and rescued him.

David's car was now in State College, and I pulled the engine. Chris and I can no longer remember which of us repaired it, but since it was in State College, and he was working at Brattleboro Tire, it seems likely that I did it. I remember vaguely the extreme wear of the holes in the flywheel into which the pins on the flange of the crankshaft fit. Chris now uses Locktite on anything like this, and doesn't worry about torque figures— he just takes it up to the yield point.

While I was working on Chris' car, he had the Spitfire again, and at about this time he went to work for a school friend, known as the Troll to all the family (but not to his face). Chris and the Troll were doing rust repair on Vermont cars, and Chris' welding skills were improving by leaps and bounds. It was the spring of '77. The Spitfire dropped a valve, which holed a piston. This gave Chris an opportunity to rebuild that engine also. While it was out of the car, he rebuilt the transmission, replacing the thrust washer for the third gear synchromesh.

He also rebuilt the Farmall M tractor engine for Elm Lea Farm in the summer of '77, installing a "Super Fire Crater Power Pack!" (or something close to that) which included high compression pistons and new jets for the carburetor, and new timing instructions. He transported the engine to Tri State Automotive in Brattleboro (for the installation of the sleeves) on the passenger seat of the Spitfire, much to the amusement of the guys at the shop, who removed it with a chain hoist. When the farm manager left Putney School, he bought the tractor, and still uses it.

Finally Chris had his car back again. He drove it for about a year, until the spring of '78. By this time, he had moved back to State College and was living with Katy and Robert. The engine began to make intermittent clicking noises. He listened carefully but couldn't detect a pattern of when it clicked and when it didn't. He was having dinner out one day when the click became a knock, and it was clear that he had lost a rod bearing. He left the car there and had a friend tow him back to Katy and Robert's a few days later. When he tore the engine apart, he found a very small blob of silicone gasket sealant trapped in the oil feed hole of one of the main bearings, and the rod bearing that was fed from it was indeed gone. He had used a liberal application of silicone sealant to stop the external oil cooler from leaking. Now, he says, he lets things like that leak as they will.

After that, David's bug was fine and reliable for many years. It made the circuit from State College to Ithaca to Vermont and back many times as Chris attended Penn State off and on, acquired a girl friend in Vermont, and eventually a wife.

Sometime in the early '80s, Chris and the car were in State College at a nursery, picking up a maple tree that Jane and I had given Katy and Robert as a present. The tree was sticking out of the sunroof, the earth ball resting on the passenger seat, with Robert and Andrew (another friend from school) in the back seat and Chris driving, when suddenly the car started to fill with smoke. For a few minutes it was a scene of acute panic as everyone tried to get out of the car at once. They found the source and extinguished the fire before any serious damage was done.

Chris had been doing some work on the windshield wipers, and had left off the pressed fiberboard cover that protected the wiring. There were loose wrenches and screwdrivers lying just in front of the wiring, and the motion of the car caused them to slide into the wiring, shorting out several terminals. The resultant heat set fire to the insulation, as well as to some trash that was just in front of the wiring.

Jennifer was still in Belgium, but she would not stay indefinitely and would need her car. After spending another year at the Institut St. Luc, she transferred to the Maryland Institute College of Art. She retrieved her car from Chris. We moved Jenny into an apartment on St. Paul Street in Baltimore, just a couple of blocks from the Hopkins campus. All of us went down for a mad weekend at the end of summer, driving a U-Haul truck that contained the furniture, and repainted her apartment from end to end.

I felt as if I had been the shop manager for a fleet of Beetles, but I did not have one for myself. In addition, I needed a car in the spring of '76, because Chris had taken the Spitfire up to Putney. Rebuilding Beetles was getting to be fun. So, I scanned the local ads and identified another 1965 Beetle. It appeared to be in reasonable condition, except for the engine, and the price was right. Again, I sent to J.C. Whitney for a maximum upgrade to 1200 cc, and this time I got a large Holley carburetor as well as the external oil cooler. This turned out to be a wonderful car, and I drove it in various incarnations for nearly 15 years.

All of these cars required a certain amount of body work, although not as much as they would when they were older. Usually there were places that had rusted through in the rear wheel wells, in the front wheel wells into the heater channels, and in the heater channels themselves. I did not yet know how to weld, or own the tools to do it. However, I devised a technique that worked very well, involving pop rivets, roofing cement and galvanized sheet. It was a messy business, and my clothes were covered with the black roofing cement, but it worked. It formed a patch that was essentially permanent, at least for the time that we owned these cars.

At about this time I received a call from Cornell, asking if I might be interested in a change of venue.

Jenny's Beetle on Chincoteague Island with a friend.

When we made our first trip to Ithaca and were given a tour by a real estate agent, she showed us a perfectly charming 1860 Victorian house with a cupola, an attached barn and a pond. We said to ourselves that if we could get the house, we would accept Cornell's offer. We did, and we did. We never told Cornell this story.

The attached barn had been used for wood storage during the house's early days, when wood was used for heating and cooking. I should have taken the opportunity to have a pit dug, so that I could work on the undersides of cars standing up, but I didn't. Either a pit or a lift would probably have been a problem, because of the layout of the barn; it would have been nearly impossible to align the car with the pit or lift without putting a wheel into the pit, or running into a lift column.

The barn connected to the basement, where the furnace was located, so there was always some heat. Someone had applied a layer of Homosote over polyethylene sheet to the inside of the barn, so there was some insulation. For the first time in my life I had a place to work out of the cold. I even installed a wood stove.

For a while my time at home was occupied with maintenance. The rear wheel arches of the Fiat rusted out, and I rebuilt them using pop rivets and galvanized sheet, tastefully faired in with body filler. With a nice paint job, it was invisible. The Fiat came with an owner's manual detailing various jobs that must be done at various mileages. The valve clearance must be adjusted at such and such a mileage, the timing belt must be replaced at 30,000 miles, and so forth. I did all these. The boots on the constant velocity joints tore and had to be replaced.

The various VWs required continuing care. The kingpins and bushings of the front torsion bar arms had to be replaced fairly often. These would last a long time if the front end were greased every 1500 miles. However, greased at the time of replacement, these were probably never greased again.

The beautiful engine in my VW only lasted 40,000 miles before throwing a rod bearing. This was traced to my failure to have the case line-reamed. So, I did the whole thing again.

The heater channels needed to be replaced, and I got Danish aftermarket parts, which I riveted in place. In a frantic effort to stop the inexorable march of rust, I took to applying roofing cement with a trowel to the entire underside of the body pan.

Jenny had spent two years at the Maryland Institute. After graduating she took a job at Ridge Runners, an outdoor outfitting store, so that she could stay in Baltimore for a while longer. It was now the summer of '79. She was still driving the blue Beetle, and it was gradually deteriorating.

Jennifer felt she was trapped in a set of unpredictable, exasperating physical circumstances, never knowing what the next difficulty would be — having to push start the car for three months, and therefore able to park only in spaces heading downhill; having to drive while wearing a goose-down sleeping bag and booties because of the lack of a heater; having to drive during a rainstorm with her head out the window because the windshield wipers were unintentionally intermittent. She felt that all these circumstances required some sort of internal emotional adjustment, and an enhanced connection with me and countless mechanics as well as with the friends who had to adjust with her (and help her push).

Besides these problems, Jenny parked by the Braille method, so that the fenders were in appalling condition. However, there was more. Once, the car stopped, and it was not immediately evident why. Eventually, it was determined that the battery (which is under the back seat) had fallen through the floor onto the road, severing its connection to the car. On a trip to New York to pick up Raymond (her Belgian boyfriend, who became her husband) she had taken a friend along for company. It was raining heavily, and every time Jenny stopped, her friend had to pick up her feet to avoid the tidal wave of water that surged forward from the back seat.

The final straw came when Jenny and Raymond drove out to Wyoming so that Jennifer could take the Outdoor Educators' Class at NOLS. The car got as far as Indiana and died. They found a garage, which decided that it needed a valve job (hardly surprising). Raymond claims that it was here that he asked Jenny to marry him; Jenny claims that it was put in such an understated way that she didn't understand the proposal, and had to have it explained to her years later. At any rate, the mechanic and I conferred by phone, and they left the car there and took a Greyhound bus to Wyoming. There Raymond camped in a pup tent in a small local park in Lander, where every evening drunken Indians would urinate on the side of his tent.

Francine and Jeff, two friends of Jenny and Raymond from Belgium, had also come over for that summer and had spent a month with them in Baltimore. They then bought a VW bug of their own and set off to tour the country. Jenny and Raymond were in touch with them, and asked them if they could give them a ride from Wyoming back to Indiana to pick up their bug. They did, and this may have been the last straw for their relationship, because shortly thereafter Francine left for Canada and Jeff went back to Belgium. Francine found her future husband Douglas in Canada on that trip, while Jeff married a Belgian girl, had a child, then put a bullet through his head.

The valve job was done when they got back to Indiana, for the price of $350 or thereabouts, which I paid. They drove the bug back to Baltimore, but it still had a serious problem, which turned out to be due to the omission of a gasket or seal (nobody remembers exactly what) by the mechanic in Indiana.

Jenny finally brought the car home for attention and opened the passenger door — there was no sill and no floor. It was almost possible to walk into the car, keeping your feet on solid ground, and sit down. This had all gradually rusted away a little at a time.

She left the car at home, and I loaned her mine. I managed to reconstruct the car from a combination of Danish patch panels, bits from the junkyard and fabricated pieces. I made an effort to bang the fenders back into some kind of shape. I also rebuilt the engine, but this was becoming almost routine.

Jenny came home and we traded cars again.

At the end of 1981, Jenny and Raymond got married in Katy and Robert's house in State College. In the summer of '83, she and Raymond went off to Belgium, where he was retreaded in computer science at the University of Liège. Raymond's program would take two years, and during this time Jenny left the blue Beetle with me.

Jenny's Beetle in Takoma Park after the Full Monty.

I decided to give it the full treatment. It had been behaving well. The engine was fine, and so were the floor and the heater channels. I did the brakes and repaired a few other places where there was rust. I put four new Brazilian fenders on it and gave it a beautiful coat of the same blue. It got new Brazilian front and rear bumpers and bumperettes, and a whole new interior with seat covers and carpets, as well as new door-seals. I also restored the windshield wipers and made sure the heater worked. It was a thing of beauty, and it was waiting for her when she and Raymond came back in the fall of '85.

They moved to Takoma Park, Maryland, while Jenny attended graduate school at American University to get an MFA. Raymond got a job as a software engineer. After about two years the engine began to make noises that suggested a thrown rod bearing. This was about eight years after I had rebuilt the engine, and it had probably acquired 80,000 miles in that period (maybe more). I simply did not have time to cope with the engine then, so I sent Jennifer home with the engine that Katy had gotten at the junkyard outside Chicago. When she took it to her mechanic, he said that they had heard her coming several blocks away, and knew exactly who it was. The mechanic looked at the engine in the back seat and said that it looked 100 years old, and that in 11 years of working there he had never seen anything like *that*. When Jenny explained that I wanted it installed, he said, "And he thinks it is going to run?" The engine left a live snake in the car, which had apparently been living happily in the engine while it was resting in our basement.

In fact, they could not get the engine to run (although it had been running when Katy came back from the West) and they could not afford to have the mechanic figure out what was wrong. They sold the car to the man across the street for $150. I hope he was very happy. Jenny and Raymond bought a real car. She says now that she has never had a car since the VW that she liked half as much.

The Spitfire had come home to roost a year or two before and had been sitting in the back yard quietly rusting. Jane threatened to fill it with soil and plant petunias in it. I had run out of things to do, and I finally decided to attack the Spitfire. On closer examination, the body was rapidly going, partly as a result of the years (it was now about 12 years old) and probably partly as a result of standing over damp soil in the backyard. Also, it was a convertible, so inevitably it had been rained into from time to time when it had been left with the top down in questionable weather. The carpets soaked up the rain and maintained a nice damp environment next to the floor. The body had a tunnel down the middle for the drive shaft, and relatively high door sills. The seats sat in wells between the drive shaft tunnel and the sills. There was not much left of these wells, either under the seats or in the footwells. Fortunately, the Spitfire had a separate frame, so that the body was not load bearing.

I fabricated new wells out of galvanized 18 gauge steel. I was disappointed to find that Chris' repairs to the rocker panels had rusted again (from the inside out, of course). I made new rocker panels.

The front fenders and hood were made in one piece, and this had survived fairly well, with little serious rust. There was some important patching to do around the rear fender wells and the trunk. When all the structural work was done, I rehung the doors and tried to roll up the windows. The doors were a tight fit; it was impossible to get the clearance right at the closing edge, but I managed to get a workable compromise. However, the windows were a serious shock to my system. The front edge of the windows interfered with the windshield posts by about a half-inch. That is, the whole windshield was now tilted back about a half-inch too far at the top.

I now know that a convertible body is structurally weak because of the absence of a top. If any structural work is done to the body, it is essential to maintain the door opening geometry and the windshield angle. This is often done by inserting a jack at an angle between the dash and a strong point somewhere near the rear seat pan. My body was probably supported by attachment points to the frame in front and back, and with the floor removed it had collapsed in the center.

Too late now. I was desperate for a solution. I finally decided on Plexiglas of the same thickness. This is street legal and can be cut to any size or shape. It is often used in convertible rear windows.

I decided to rustproof the car (it certainly needed it). Rustproofing had been just coming on the market when we had been on sabbatical. When the Fiat was new, in the fall of 1973, we had had it rustproofed in Belgium, using a Swedish process (now used by everyone, as far as I can tell). However, this was about 1980, and it was not yet possible to buy rustproofing apparatus for use at home. I went to our local petroleum products supplier and found that he could supply 25 gallon drums of rustproofing from Texaco. I got one. It was amazingly cheap. I still have about half of it — it will never decay or deteriorate. I use a little from time to time. I intend to will the remainder to my children. The rustproofing is probably the discard from distilling crude petroleum; it is somewhere between a grease and a wax. What a bonanza it must have been for the refiners, to have a new market for this awkward substance. However, I had to apply it somehow. I had had enough of applying thick goop with a trowel and, besides, I wanted to spray it inside panels. I diluted the muck with wax and grease remover (after all, I did not want it to dissolve paint), and made a three-foot-long wand with a nozzle and aspirator at the end. It worked splendidly, and for quite a few years I sprayed it inside nearly everything I worked on. Now, I am afraid I buy commercial stuff, which is less messy, and I have a professional cavity wand to get inside doors and the like. However, my jury-rig was quite satisfactory at the time.

I gave the car a nice coat of paint in Signal Red, the original color. The body work that showed was less than professional: I had had almost no experience with block sanding and feathering, so the filler was visible under the paint. However, the overall appearance was satisfactory. It was what I have learned to call a ten-foot job; that is, it looked good from ten feet away. The upholstery on the seats was very far gone. They could have been reupholstered, and I would later do this kind of work, but the car was not worth the effort. I got a pair of cheap fiberglass seats from J.C. Whitney, and they looked fine. I got new carpet and a new top. Chris had rebuilt the engine while he had had the car up at Putney, so it was now a virtually new car. Sort of.

I drove it for a while, but I had my eye on bigger game. I wanted to sell the Spitfire and get something more interesting to restore. I advertised the Spitfire in all the likely places. I had an idea of what it might be worth, but that evidently did not agree with other people's ideas. I lowered the price little by little. No nibbles. We had a young man working for us from time to time, Jim Merod, the son of my secretary. He was bright and brash. He had the idea of taking the Spitfire down to the local baseball game and parking it in a place where it would be seen by the fans as they streamed out of the ball park after the game. That didn't work either. Finally, as the price came inexorably down each week, we had a nibble. The local director of the FBI bought the car and drove it for several years. I saw him from time to time professionally, when he came to my office to do background checks on students who wanted a job with the federal government. I always asked about the car, not out of nostalgia, but to learn how well the restoration was holding up. I also needed to find out how much the car had blackened my reputation, although I didn't really want to know. Sort of like picking at a scab.

At about this time I had Jim insulate the barn properly. The two sliding barn doors were permanently closed up and insulated. After a winter in which I tried to insulate the original wooden garage door with panels of rigid insulation, I bought an insulated modern garage door and installed it.

I had bought an air compressor when I started working on Beetles, a relatively inexpensive one from Sears, Roebuck. That was fine for a while, but it became evident that it was not large enough. When we moved to Ithaca I bought a larger one, also from Sears. I was now using a few air tools. The new compressor was adequate for a while, but it was becoming evident that it was not large enough. Hadn't we been here before? I finally got serious and got a truly large industrial air compressor, four cylinder, five horsepower, with a 120 gallon tank. I permanently plumbed it in, with copper piping, pitched so that condensation would run back to the tank, with a trap and a filter at each of two outlets. This has proven satisfactory, but it could still stand to be bigger.

Around 1983 Chris brought his Beetle home for a face lift and paint job. It needed substantial rust repair in all the usual places. He fabricated all the necessary patch panels and welded them in place, doing a beautiful job. This was the first real test of the new air compressor. We were still using the wood stove in the barn, while Chris was spraying paint. I had theories about why this was relatively safe, but they are not something in which I have a lot of confidence. It was probably just luck that we were not blown up. At any rate, the paint job turned out very nicely — a lovely shade of dark green, a little lighter than British Racing Green.

Chris drove this car happily until 1987, when he sold it to a school friend for $250.

In 1983 Chris also brought home Robert's (Katy's husband) van, which he had agreed to paint after doing all necessary body work. This was an aging vehicle, and there was a lot of rust. Chris cut out all the bad parts, welded in patches, faired them in with filler, and then painted the van. It looked very nice, but the job didn't last — little water-filled blisters began forming within a year, a sign of rusting through from the back, suggesting that much of the apparently sound sheet metal was close to perforation when Chris patched it.

Finally, Chris offered to paint my Beetle in compensation for occupying my barn for so long. My Beetle had always been black and was now looking pretty disreputable. We decided on black again. He did a splendid job, and it looked gorgeous. I drove this Beetle until the early nineties, taking it nearly everywhere — to out of town meetings within 300 miles, so to Bethlehem, Boston, and Rochester. It was absolutely reliable, fast and handled well. For a while it suffered from carburetor icing because the arrangement to bring exhaust gases to heat the intake manifold was plugged, but that was soon fixed.

One day Jane borrowed my Beetle to drive over to school. When she pulled into the school parking lot and applied the brakes, nothing happened. The car was headed straight for the front door of Upson Hall. She managed to turn left, up over the sidewalk, and into a rail fence and a hedge before she came to a stop. It turned out that the brake line had rusted through inside the passenger compartment, where it lies along the side of the tunnel that contains the shift mechanism. It had been kept nice and wet in winter by the sodden carpet. After I diagnosed the problem, I left the car standing in the yard, waiting until I had time to fix it. In the meantime its registration came due, and I did not renew it. One day we received a notice from the town supervisors to the effect that it had been observed that we had an unregistered, derelict vehicle standing on our property in public view, and we had 30 days to remove it or it would be removed by the town. This seemed a bit much — I have always suspected that the town supervisor's brother-in-law ran a towing service. But, maybe not. In any event, it was midwinter, both bays in the barn were occupied, and I did not have the time or inclination to strip out the brake lines and replace them just then. We advertised the Beetle and got a buyer almost immediately. He took it away and then came back a few days later to say that although he had not believed me when I told him all the things that I had done to the car, he was amazed to find it was all true and then some. And, he wanted to return an air wrench that I had been looking for, which had been on top of the gas tank in the trunk.

Chapter 10

Armstrong Siddeley

MY APPETITE HAD BEEN whetted by the amateur restorations I had done on Jenny's Beetle and the Spitfire, and I now wanted to do something real. I subscribed to *Hemmings Motor News* and read it assiduously every month. *Hemmings* is a collection of classified ads, organized into sections of services offered, supplies, tools for sale, "A" cars, "B" cars, and so forth. Some 800 pages of it arrive every month. It is read and used by everyone with an old car hobby. I was looking specifically for something mechanically and historically interesting, but an orphan, so that it would not be too expensive. By orphan, I mean an off-brand, a make not well known.

I came across a cryptic ad for an Armstrong Siddeley. I had never heard of this make. I tried to find out about it, but it proved to be difficult. I did not have an extensive library of car books, but I went through the indices of everything available at the local bookstore. Finally in one of these I found a reference suggesting that Armstrong Siddeley had been regarded as a prestigious make at one time.

I talked to the owner. The car had been repossessed at some point in the past, and had sat in a repossession yard in Queens, in New York City. Cars are stored in these yards until someone pays what is owed on them. They stand outside in all weather. Eventually, if they are not adopted, they are auctioned off, but by that time they have usually been nearly destroyed by the summer heat. The owner had attended the auction, and had bid on the car, and it was now in his garage, also in Queens.

I thought I would call my friend in New York City, David Keller. David and his wife Joanie spent summers in Ithaca, where David taught in a writing program with my wife. My interaction with them had to do with eating and drinking. David loved good food and good wine, and every summer a number of parties would be arranged for the people in the writing program. David played the piano at a professional level, and the parties usually ended with an impromptu concert by David.

I have to explain that David was a classic New York City type. I am sure that he had never changed a faucet washer in his life, and perhaps not even a light bulb. He normally did not drive, although he could. When he first came to Ithaca, he told his son frequently, "Don't touch that! You don't know where it's been." He was accustomed to living in a building with a doorman and a super, and garbage collection, where all the needs of life were taken care of by invisible people. Otherwise, David was a large, warm, gentle man. Joanie had a similar background, but it was combined with a very savvy, tough, street-smart, no-nonsense personality in an attractive petite package.

These were the people I called to go and check out this Armstrong Siddeley. David sounded horrified at the thought of going to Queens from Brooklyn. I had the impression that Queens was not a place where one went. He was clearly struggling, trying to balance his loyalty to me with his revulsion at the thought. When he told Joanie what he was about to do, I am sure he got an earful.

However, David went, and he took his Polaroid camera. He took a number of clear pictures of the car, inside and out, and of the engine compartment, as it stood in a garage in Queens. I can only visualize his horror. Of course, the car was in terrible condition. There had been no maintenance on the car for years before it had been sent to the repo lot, and sitting there exposed had done it no good. The leather upholstery was dried out and badly split. The carpets were worn and dirty. The woodwork was delaminating, and the veneer peeling off. The engine compartment was filthy, with many nonstandard, jury-rigged bits and pieces here and there. There was a great deal of rust in the lower six inches all the way around the body, but I doubt that David saw that. He saw a filthy mess, and I am sure felt that any normal person would send it to the crusher and wash his hands of it. The thought that I would actually see something desirable here, and want to be involved with it, must have struck him as demented.

I called the owner and made an offer of $750. From the alacrity with which he accepted, I gathered my offer was far more than he expected. I arranged for a roll-back to drive down from Ithaca to pick up the Armstrong Siddeley. I got a frantic phone call from the owner when the roll-back arrived, asking for verification that it was really representing me — I couldn't imagine who he thought might have engineered a clandestine plot to carnap the vehicle. Later that day the rollback pulled up to our garage door. The Armstrong Siddeley was gorgeous to my eyes. It was a very dirty British Racing Green, and had an imposing vertical grill; the front and rear fenders formed a beautiful swoopy line. The driver said that he had had a number of friendly waves and yells from passing drivers, asking what it was.

What I had bought was called by the factory a Sapphire 346, because it had a 3.4 liter displacement and six cylinders. It had been built in 1954, so it was the same age as my oldest child, Katy. It was the first new postwar design that Armstrong Siddeley produced. W.O. Bentley had been hired as a consultant on the engine, and he had recommended that they consider a double overhead camshaft. That proved to be too noisy and too expensive, and W.O. was fired, and this overhead valve engine with push rods was designed in house.

A friend was up for the weekend, and together we got out the crank and determined that the engine was free. It would need a battery before I could consider the possibility of starting it. I got a battery the next day. The only battery that would fit was a deep-cycle boat battery. The guy at Sears tried to give me a hard time, wanting to know what boat it was going in, and then telling me it was totally inappropriate for a vehicle. In fact, it had approximately the ampere-hour rating that the manufacturer had specified. Deep cycle was an excellent idea. Batteries that are used in contemporary cars are not designed to be completely discharged and recharged. I don't know what happens to their interiors, but a couple of cycles of this and the battery is ruined. With an old car, the car is put to bed every year before the first snow, perhaps in October, and then is brought out again in May after the last snow. The old car magazines tell you to take the battery out, bring it inside to a warm place and keep it on charge all winter. I am sure that is good advice. But batteries of this size weigh about 50 pounds, and it is very awkward horsing them out of and back into the car, especially as the enthusiast ages. I leave the battery right where it belongs, as most boat owners do. There is usually slow leakage over the winter, so that the battery is somewhat run down by spring. Usually, there is enough oomph left to start the car.

For a wonder, the engine started, although it was clear that it needed a lot of tender loving care. However, there were no serious noises, no heavy knocks indicating destroyed connecting rods or main bearings. There was a persistent squeak-squeak-squeak that I traced to the distributor drive shaft, which had a grease cup that had not been refilled in decades.

Although I was itching to begin on the car, I needed literature, specifically a shop manual and a parts list at a minimum. I spent the time taking roll after roll of Polaroid pictures of every conceivable part of the car, so that I would be able to remember how things had been when it came time to put it back together. I am sometimes tempted to abbreviate this process, being sure I will remember everything. When I was 16, I could just throw all the small parts in a bucket for cleaning, and never had any problem identifying the proper destination of every nut and bolt. I have always flattered myself, thinking of this as something like what a chess master does, who can play two dozen simultaneous games, remembering all the positions. However, that was when I was 16. Up until recently I could still put down a tool and walk away, and remember an hour later where I had put it down. No more. Now I have to clean up every so often, putting everything away, in order to find things. And, I definitely need the pictures. I remember in an approximate way, but the devil is in the details.

I was reading everything on restoration that I could lay my hands on. I had a couple of British car magazines, one aimed specifically at home restorers. I also bought several books on restoration. The more specialized ones, on sheet metal work, painting, upholstery and so forth, were very helpful.

One of the car magazines had a list of owners' clubs. I found a UK club for the Armstrong Siddeley and wrote to them. What a wonderful club! And, what a bonanza! I have since discovered that this club is remarkable in a number of respects. When the factory closed its doors in 1960, the club was formed and bought the factory's stock of parts. The perishable parts, of course, have long since perished, but they have all the imperishable ones. In addition, they have had a number of the perishable ones produced. They have reproduced all the literature, and have available the shop manuals, the parts lists, the manufacturer's advisories, even little booklets on the door locks, the heater, the distributor and so forth.

For a wonder, they also have available the factory files on many of the cars. When the factory closed, the new owners decided to clean out all these old files, dumped them in a huge pile in the courtyard, and lit a bonfire. At that moment a representative of the new owners' club came buy, saw what was happening with horror, grabbed a rake, and began pulling files from the bonfire. About half the files were saved. These files contain all the memos defining the car when it was ordered: each memo is a change order, countersigned by the shop foreman, specifying a change to the ducting, the upholstery, the front floor, or other detail. Then there is a copy of the bill of sale forwarded to the dealer, and the bill of lading from when the car was shipped. Following this, there are copies of all the letters between the new owner and the factory, ordering parts, asking for information, and so forth.

Unfortunately, I could not have this treasure trove for this car. Its file was one of those that had been burnt in the courtyard.

The restoration was just beginning. I did not yet realize that it is a good idea to strip it all down first.

With the shop manual and parts book in hand, I began to dismantle the car. As I worked my way through it, I kept lists of parts that would be needed. Many parts were clearly worn out, or had not been maintained, or had been consumed by rust. There were, of course, many perishable parts, such as rubber suspension bushings, that needed to be replaced. I found under the car great quantities of sandy loam. I speculated that the car had been used on a farm out on Long Island. The rear brakes had failed, and someone had cut off the brake lines and rolled them up like the bottom of a toothpaste tube to seal them, leaving the car with front brakes only.

I needed parts for the engine, of course. It was in reasonably good condition, and did not need to go to the machine shop. It did need the consumable parts. Many trim pieces were needed, and many of the internal door and window handles were broken.

When I had a reasonably complete list, I sent it to the stores maintained by the owners' club. I waited. And waited. I wrote again, reminding the stores person of my previous list, and adding a few items. Still no answer. I called, and spoke to the person, named Martin Hawker. He was very cordial, and assured me that he had my order and would send my parts forthwith. Still nothing. I called again. Still nothing. I wrote to one of the club directors who oversaw the parts operation, and complained. He reassured me, but still nothing happened. From letters exchanged with other members, I learned that Martin Hawker was a former swineherd who knew little about cars and was not especially fond of work.

At the annual general meeting of the club, the problem of Martin Hawker was brought up. This polarized the club into a pro–Martin group and an anti–Martin group. The people trying to ease Martin out were accused of all sorts of insensitivity and vindictiveness. I did not know any of these people, but I could only assume that the pro–Martin people were his old buddies, for whom he actually produced parts. I have since learned that owners' clubs often have these internal battles. It seemed to me remarkably nasty, and in the long run resulted in major changes in the board of directors.

Getting my parts was proving to be more difficult than I had imagined. Fortunately, I had a scientific meeting in Europe at about that time, and when the meeting was over, I arranged to stop over for a few days in England and drive down to Conkwell Farm, Bradford-on-Avon, Wiltshire. The parts were stored at that time in a group of sheds with leaking roofs. I had made arrangements to meet Martin at the stores (he normally came in only a couple of days a week). Martin was a friendly fellow, and with me there to follow him around, we got a lot done. I spent the entire day, and we managed to find and pull every part I needed, making a great pile on the floor near the front door. It was with considerable misgivings that I left the parts there — if I could have taken them home with me on the airplane I would have been much happier — but Martin did actually send them to me after a reasonable delay.

The body was not as good as it had looked when I first saw it. Closer inspection showed that the bottom six inches of the car all the way around (and a few other places besides) was held together mostly by paint.

I still did not know how to weld. I bought a large professional welding machine and started practicing. I was awful. I should have taken a course at the local trade school, but in the tradition of men who refuse to ask directions when they are lost, I insisted on teaching myself. Fortunately Christopher knew how to weld, and enlightened me about several tricks of the trade.

The sills were large box sections that ran along the sides of the body, underneath the doors. They had been designed with large lightening holes in the inner surface but no drain holes in the bottom. As a result, they would fill with water and road salt up to the bottom of the lightening holes

The new sills, and the side of the scuttle. Note the amateur welding.

and rapidly rust through. The replacement sills were the first things I ever welded. After restoring the car, I drove it for 12 years, anxiously waiting for one of my welds to fail, but none ever did.

I also had to replace the rear inner fender wells, which formed the sides of the trunk.

I used brazing on some of the thin sheet metal, because I did not trust my welding. I also did a number of amateur things that made my life more difficult.

I was helped a great deal by Penn Bradley, the historian of the Australian Armstrong Siddeley Car Club. Although his technical training is minimal, he has an encyclopedic mind. He remembers details (even down to part numbers) the way some enthusiasts remember baseball statistics. My car was a left-hand drive, and consequently several items were specific to that car. The owners' club in the UK no longer had these left-hand drive parts, if they had ever had them, because so few left-hand drive cars had been produced. At one point I told Penn that I was not having any success finding a left-hand drive parking brake cable, and he asked me the part number. He immediately recognized the part number as being the same as a right-hand drive parking brake cable from a much earlier model, which had been remanufactured by the Aussies.

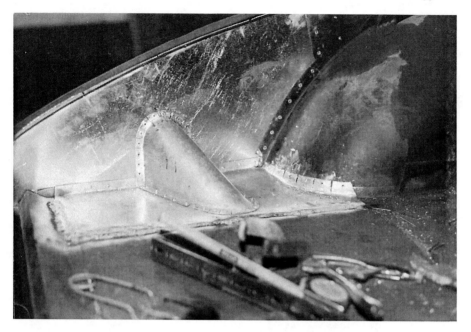

The left side inner fender well and gas filler. Note I am using lots of pop rivets to avoid difficult welding, and I have snipped the turnup to avoid stretching with hammer and dolley.

We exchanged many, many letters, in which Penn told me Armstrong Siddeley war stories and gave me advice on the restoration, relaying the experience of other restorers. There is now (in 2001) an Internet mailing list for Armstrong Siddeley enthusiasts, by which they can exchange e-mail about their restoration problems. This did not exist at the time of my project, and Penn served that purpose. According to Penn, Armstrong Siddeleys in Australia get hard usage. They are driven at 80 miles an hour on gravel roads in the outback, accumulating a quarter million miles, barely slowing down to cross dried stream beds, being stopped only by accidentally running down the stray kangaroo. In this story, the kangaroo body became wedged in the right front wheel well and caused the car to flip end-over-end. The car was repaired and still exists in the owners' club in Oz. Penn is the author of at least one book on the postwar Armstrong Siddeley.

Slowly, slowly, I worked my way through the entire car. When all the body work had been repaired, I began surface preparation for painting.

I was going to use lacquer and a lacquer-based primer. This was not a good choice, although it is easy to work with. It means that there is a

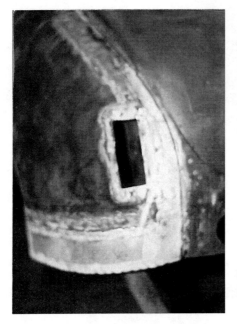 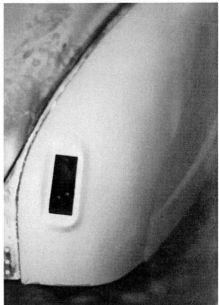

Left: The left rear fender after replacing the taillight surround, the bolting flange and the lower edge. Note the brazing. *Right:* The right rear fender in primer; this had been in a condition similar to the other side.

wait of several weeks between operations, to allow the solvents to evaporate. It was painfully tedious work.

I had to take a few days off to go to Putney, Vermont, to get Christopher properly married to Melissa. Back in Ithaca after the wedding, it was finally time for paint. This is a terribly exciting part of any restoration. After all the hard, filthy work, at last there is something beautiful.

The car had originally been a color the manufacturer called Corinthian Green, no longer available. I had one good rear door panel from which I was able to sand off the British Racing Green, down to the original Corinthian Green; by a fairly organized process, I was able to match this.

When the paint was finally sanded and compounded, it was beautiful beyond my wildest dreams. It was a lovely color, and the repair work was invisible: the flat panels looked flat, no ripples were visible, and it had a deep, clear gloss. Now it needed a coachline.

When the car had left the factory, it had had a hand-painted coach line. There are descriptions in the literature provided by the owner's club of the application of this coach line, which ran along the edge of the hood,

The restored engine. Note red firewall, an amateur choice; also the anachronistic throttle control cable and modern coil, all deductions in judging.

beneath the windows, and down the edge of the trunk, from one end of the car to the other. In the factory there had been an elderly man with a bench covered with partially used pots of various colors, and jars of delicate brushes, and a burner and kettle for making tea. He constantly sipped at a tea mug, and his hands had a fine tremor from the level of caffeine in his system. When a body was pushed up to his station, however, and he took up a brush and dipped it in the appropriate paint pot, the tremor vanished, and in one smooth movement he painted a line down the entire side of the car.

My car had a triple line: a thin stripe of red, with a thin stripe of yellow on each side. When the car was repainted, these had been carefully masked off to preserve them. Now I had to reproduce them. I am afraid I used a tiny roller, instead of learning how to do it with a brush. With a lot of fear and trembling and lots of wiping off and starting again, I managed to do a pretty good job. There were a couple of places where the work might have been improved, but it looked very nice from a couple of feet away.

The first order of business in the interior was the door panels. These were built up using a piece of very thin plywood with a stiffening frame

The body in primer. Spray it on and sand it off. Spray it on and sand it off …

screwed to the panel, all covered with vinyl (Armstrong Siddeley cut costs by using leather on the seats where it counted, but vinyl on the backs of the seats and on the door panels). The vinyl was held in place using glue and staples. The hardest part of the whole operation was finding staples that would not penetrate the thin plywood, and stapling guns and pliers to apply them. I finally found that there are staple specialists, as there are for everything else, and I got exactly what I needed.

The next order of business in the interior was the wood trim. The door cappings and dash were veneered with walnut burl. The veneer was peeling off in many places and needed to be replaced. To begin with, I was unsure what the veneer was. I had a number of informal opinions, but there was no reason to believe any of the commentators. At one point, I took it to a woodworker recommended by some friends who had a boat. This man did repairs to local boats. He was a sweet little old man. I explained my problem to him, and he agreed to give it a try. Did I have a sample? I had brought a door capping. He took it and began to delicately work at it with a scraper. I assumed that he was removing the finish, to see the wood more clearly. There was not much finish on it, but that made sense. However, he continued, and I could see that he was now removing the veneer. I feebly remonstrated, but he reassured me that he just needed to get the finish off, so that he could see the grain of the wood. Finally, when he had completely removed the veneer, he declared it to be a nice piece of mahogany. I thanked him very much for his time, paid him, and got out of there. He was as blind as a bat, and could not see well enough to tell what was veneer and what was finish. I finally found out from the owner's club what I should have suspected in the beginning, that the veneer was good English walnut burl.

A burl is a sort of tumor that attacks a tree, growing chaotically, producing a great lump sometimes several feet in diameter, which can be sliced into veneer. I called various suppliers to try to obtain walnut burl veneer. I called a number in New York City and got a bored voice. When I explained to him what I wanted, he asked me how much I needed. I told him how many square feet, and there was a silence at the other end of the phone. Then he gently explained to me that they sold only by the flitch. What is a flitch? I asked. He explained that if you start with an entire burl and slice it into veneer, that stack of veneer is a flitch. A flitch might contain 50 square yards. Fortunately, he was able to give me the name of someone who sold veneer at retail. The veneer I obtained was beautiful, thick, flame-grained walnut burl.

I reveneered and refinished all the wood. Some of the base wood was exposed (not covered with veneer), and it varied widely in color. I used a tinted lacquer (I was finishing the wood in lacquer) on this part. In the factory the worker had two spray guns, one filled with clear and the other with tinted, and he mixed coats of the two to obtain a consistent color. I did more or less the same thing.

Now, I had the entire interior to trim. This involved upholstery, door panels, head lining and carpets. The head lining was not particularly tricky, but there was an inherent problem. The lining had seams that ran from side to side. When you opened one of the front or rear doors, your eye was aligned with one of these seams. If it is not perfectly straight, it is very evident. I had to hang the head lining five times before I got the seams straight enough to suit me.

I had bought a reconditioned, used, upholstery sewing machine, with a walking foot. That is, the upper foot picks itself up and takes a step forward each time the pad in the sole plate moves, so that the fabric is propelled not just from the bottom but from the top; this enables five layers of leather and one of cotton batting to feed uniformly. I am sure this machine started life as a treadle machine, but it had been converted to power. The machine was probably older than I am.

I had learned to sew on a treadle machine. When we were first married,

The interior during trimming out. Dash, door capping and door panel.

Jane and I had bought such a machine at a junk store. Jane's mother had always had one, and Jane was quite familiar with them. For Christmas we made doll clothes for the kids, and that was how I learned to sew. I felt quite at home on the upholstery machine.

Unfortunately, leather is not as forgiving as fabric; if you go off the line and have to pull the stitches out, they leave a line of little holes in the leather that cannot be hidden.

Most of the upholstery had to be fitted several times to get it right. The original had been too far gone to be used as more than a general guide.

The edges of the carpet had to be bound. This involved dealing with large, stiff pieces of carpet that would not fit under the throat of the machine, and folding the binding so that it would go around tight inside corners.

One of the fun parts of doing a restoration is showing it off to dinner guests. The early stages are not of much general interest. Only another car nut is interested in seeing the progress of the welding. However, as soon as the car is in paint and the interior trimming is started, the women (and the nonmechanical men) are much more interested. They love to sit in it and fantasize, like customers at an upscale dealer. Some of the comments are startling. I overheard two women sitting in the front seat commenting sotto voce that the switch for the Wilson Preselector would make a great vibrator!

The trim piece around the rear window was grained. During the Depression, when my father was super of the apartment building in Brookline, he had learned how to grain wood from one of the Italian artisans. He taught me when I was young. A pale base coat is applied. When that is dry, a much darker top coat is applied, and a turkey feather is used to make patterns, partially removing the dark top coat to reveal the lighter base coat. The edge of the feather can be snipped with scissors to make more interesting patterns. If you don't like the pattern, you can wipe it off and try again. When you are happy, let it dry, and then apply several coats of varnish to adjust the contrast (initially the contrast between the base coat and the top coat will be too great).

The glove box and the pockets in the doors were lined with flock. Flock is chopped hair or fiber; it is blown onto a tacky base to form a furry surface. It is used for small toy animals, as well as glove boxes. Initially, I tried to find flock at all sorts of inappropriate places. I remember going into the art department of the campus store and asking, "Flock?" The counter person looked at me quizzically for a moment, and said, "As in sheep?" I finally did find flock and sizing.

I had gotten new interior door handles from the owners' club. They were a little heavier than the originals, which had been too fragile. These seemed as though they should last longer. Unfortunately, they were a little larger in diameter at the point where they were to pass through the escutcheons. My escutcheons (45-year-old plastic at the time) were largely broken in any event, and those that remained were too brittle with age to be bored out. My technician, who had been with me at Penn State and Cornell for 25 years, volunteered to make new escutcheons out of white nylon. These were beautiful, but too white. The color we needed was closer to the color of old ivory. I tried a number of things, but nothing seemed to be absorbed by the nylon. Finally Jane suggested onion skins. I prepared a pot of onion skins and water, and gently boiled the escutcheons in it for several hours. They got darker and darker, and finally exactly the right shade.

The windshield is held by an extruded rubber weather strip in a chrome frame; the gap between the chrome frame and the body is sealed by another extruded rubber weather strip. The doors also seal against the body by extruded rubber weather strip, partly in foam rubber, partly not. I discovered that most of these extruded rubber parts were no longer available. I searched through the catalogs of companies that make reproduction rubber parts, but with no success. Each extruded cross section is designed specifically for the particular application. It is remarkable how different they all are. You would think that in a rational world, the rubber extruders would make a selection of cross sections, and the car designers would design their vehicles to use them, so that all cars would use the same sections. Evidently that would be too simple. Instead, the car designers design their cars with a total disregard for the sections available, and then design a section to fit. Sections are reproduced for old cars that exist in large numbers, like Fords, but the Armstrong Siddeley exists in such small numbers that it has not been worth anyone's while to do this.

I contacted a company in California that extrudes rubber sections. They were willing to make an extrusion die by hand for about $100.

Having the die made was painful. I sent the company a carefully drawn outline of what I wanted; they made the die, and returned a few test feet of extrusion. The cross section of the extrusion was like a caricature of the section I had drawn. I sent back drawings indicating how the profile should be modified. The next trial extrusion was different, but not necessarily better. As the number of iterations increased, there was a clear reluctance to continue this process. The charge for the die was fixed, and the more iterations, the more it cost the company. I was not happy. I was sympathetic to the economics of the situation, and also to the difficulty of shaping the die by hand with a file, but I was also dissatisfied with the result.

For this first car, I eventually obtained sections that I thought were adequate before the extrusion company bailed out of the process. Later I began to experiment with other possibilities.

In the shop at Cornell we managed to cut perfect dies in just a few minutes using a computer controlled milling machine. One of the advantages of using the computer controlled milling machine is that one can start with a drawing. The owners' club has factory drawings of these sections.

Why was I doing all this? I did not need these sections for my car. The sections I had were adequate, although they could certainly have been improved by this process. However, the Armstrong Siddeley owners' clubs in the UK, New Zealand and Australia were desperate for these extruded sections and I (with the help of Cornell) am now the world supplier for these owners' clubs.

The car was ready for its chrome. There was a considerable amount of it, since the window frames were chromed brass, as well as the exterior door handles, the radiator shell, parking lights and various trim pieces. I had seen ads for a company in *Hemmings Motor News*. Why I picked that company is a mystery — there are dozens advertised in *HMN*. The person I spoke with asked me to describe the car, and the pieces and their state. He then gave me a list of typical prices, so much for a door handle, so much for a grill bar, and so on. We added everything up and came to a price between $1500 and $2000. He indicated that this was more or less typical. Although this seemed high to me, I suspected I had little choice.

A few days later I shipped them the pieces by Greyhound, because the package was too large to go by UPS. I started calling daily as we got to the estimated time of arrival of the package. I talked to the same man I had spoken with previously, as well as a woman, who both assured me there was no problem sending someone over to pick up the shipment from Greyhound. By the fourth call, the shipment had arrived, but no truck was available to pick it up. He promised to send a truck for it the following day, which was Friday, or on Monday.

A week went by, and I called again, wanting a firm price. They had no record of the shipment, and both the people with whom I had previously spoken were no longer with the company. I went into cardiac arrest. I asked to speak with the boss. The boss was a former field rep who had been elevated to that position when the previous boss had been let go. At this point I was beginning to have grave misgivings. The shipment was located at the Greyhound terminal, and they agreed to send a truck for it and to prepare a firm price invoice. After about a week, I received the invoice, which was for $4,291.61. Most of the prices were about double those that had been given to me over the phone. I had been in shock at the previous price — now I was beyond help.

I called them and explained that that was more than I wanted to pay, and asked them to repack my parts and send them back to me. I agreed to pay shipping and handling, plus charges for photography (they claimed to have photographed the parts as they unpacked them). I was assured that the parts would leave that day.

Two days later, I got a call from the boss. He offered to reduce the price by $1000. I declined. He asked if I would not like them to do some few pieces, so that I could see the quality of their work. I said that I had thought of having them do the radiator shell and grill, but that their price of $1025 for this was much more than I wished to pay. The boss indicated that the parts had not yet been shipped. I asked again that they be packed and shipped as soon as possible. This was Friday. I called again on Tuesday, and found that the parts still had not been shipped. They agreed to ship the parts that day, and to call me when they had been shipped. By 4:30, they had not called, so I called them. Two-thirds of the parts had been shipped, but not to the address that I had requested. They promised to ship the remaining third the following day.

I did receive all the parts. I eventually had them chromed at a local place in Syracuse. This place had little experience of automotive parts and made a number of serious mistakes. I was so disgusted with the whole plating process, that I decided to live with the result. I could not bear the thought of going around again. At least, they were cheap.

This car had a most unusual transmission. It is called a Wilson Preselector and is an ancestor of the automatic transmission. In the Wilson Preselector, the operator controls the shifts. This is done with a switch, which resembles a miniature gearshift. This switch is placed in the appropriate gear, but nothing happens immediately. There is a pedal in the position of a clutch pedal, but this is not a clutch; it is the gearshift pedal. When the gear is wanted (having been selected by the switch), the pedal is depressed and released, and this tightens the appropriate band, engaging the selected gear. When neutral is selected, the transmission in fact tries to engage both first and reverse simultaneously. The bands cannot both be tightened, so each is about half-tightened, so they both slip, and this produces neutral. The clutch is a centrifugal clutch, called the Newton Traffic clutch. In the early days, the preselector mechanism was mechanical, looking like the selector lever on a modern automatic transmission.

The car was now essentially done, and beautiful. When it came time to start the engine for the first time in two years, I had evidently not adjusted the bands in the transmission correctly. Although it was in neutral, the first brake band was tighter than the reverse brake band, and the car surged forward into the edge of the workbench, smashing the center bar of the grill. I had been so excited I had not thought to set the parking brake. The brakes had not been bled completely, so there were no foot brakes to speak of. The driver's door was open (these are suicide doors, opening forward) and hit the edge of another bench, buckling the door at the lower hinge. This was the Friday before Christmas, with the entire family coming home, and everyone hoping for a ride in the Armstrong Siddeley. I was devastated.

The day before Christmas, everyone got rides anyhow, in the poor damaged and unregistered car (but not very far from the house). Fortunately, the owners' club had another grill center bar, and by mid–January I had managed to repair the grill and the door so that the damage was invisible to everyone but me.

The transmission was a more complicated question. All I had done previously was to clean it up. Now I felt it needed a major overhaul. Fortunately, it can be removed without removing the engine. However, I had to do this from inside the car, using an engine crane. This is a very large transmission. I was in a terrible state of anxiety, lifting it out past the new veneer on the dash, the new carpets and the new upholstery, but I managed to get it out (and back in) without damaging anything. When I dismantled it, I found that the inside of the case had been painted at the factory with a glossy orange sealer. Some additive in the oil I was using had removed this coating, and large pieces were floating in the oil and had gotten into the mechanism, gumming up the brake bands. I did what was necessary to the transmission and to the clutch while I was at it. I found that the engagement springs had been overheated at some time in the past (as though someone had used the car to pull stumps), and they had all collapsed.

I ordered a set of springs from Martin Hawker, the parts man at the Armstrong Siddeley Owner's Club. The springs did not arrive. I called again and was assured that they were on their way, by air mail. After five or six weeks, I couldn't stand it any longer. I stretched and heat treated the original springs and reassembled everything. The springs took seven weeks to arrive. They had been mailed *after* my second call, and by surface post, while I had been charged the air rate. To add insult to injury, the springs Martin sent were the wrong ones. On that occasion I offered Martin a bribe, in the form of a check for five pounds sterling for each correct part that arrived within eight days of the order. He never responded.

I assiduously studied the manual on adjustment of the transmission, and spent several days adjusting it absolutely according to Hoyle. After that, it behaved beautifully the whole time I owned the car, more than ten years. The home heat-treated springs also performed perfectly.

These restorations take a long time. I had been working on this for three years. When the car was done, I discovered that the brakes, which had been done meticulously two years before and, of course, never used, had again corroded and had to be redone. I had not used silicone brake fluid as I do now, and that was part of the problem. Ordinary brake fluid also acts as paint remover, and when the wheel cylinders leaked, it removed all the paint from the brake backing plates.

The car was finally on the road. Now new problems surfaced. There was a persistent squeal, but this was not serious. More serious was some intermittent overheating. Sometimes it would overheat at idle, sometimes at speed. As it heated up, it would burp up a quantity of fluid. In my perplexity I tried absolutely everything. I have in my notes two pages, single spaced; a detailed log of exactly what happened when, and what I did in an attempt to make sense of the situation. I changed from water to antifreeze and back (water is a better coolant, but antifreeze has a higher boiling point), I used various flushes, I backflushed. Nothing seemed to influence it, and nothing made sense. I was in anguish. Every time I made a change, I took the car out on a test circuit. Each time it overheated, and I had to pull to the side of the road and wait for it to cool down. As I sat and waited, I felt like a teenager again, when I had had similar problems with the Nash. Also, every time something went wrong, there was the possibility of damaging the beautiful restoration.

At the same time I was considering other possibilities—there were at least four or five, and I checked them all, some several times. Several of these required removing the grill and radiator, as well as the water pump, with the possibility of damaging the new paint and the new chrome. I replaced several parts, which considerably improved the performance of the engine but had no effect on the overheating problem. Finally, I removed the water pump one last time, and discovered that the problem was with the water pump impeller, which pushes the cooling water around. It was supposed to be a press fit on the shaft, but was loose. I fixed it with belt *and* suspenders, and it has been fine ever since.

The squeal was less serious, but even more elusive. Squeals are very hard to locate, because their high pitch makes them bounce off anything metallic. It was clear it was from the front of the engine, but beyond that nothing was clear. I thought it was the water pump bearing. I replaced it. That wasn't it. It would have been a help if it had been consistent, but it was an off-again on-again sort of thing, so each time I could believe for a while that maybe I had got it. I thought it was the generator bearing. I dismantled the generator and replaced the bearings. No, again. It seemed to be affected by tightening and loosening the fan belt, which suggested all kinds of things. I found a series of four Technical Data and Service Bulletins from 1955 and early 1956 dealing with squeaking water pumps. From the variety of solutions recommended and withdrawn, it was evident that this had been a persistent problem, which the factory had not been able to resolve definitively. I reduced it to a chirp on starting, and no squeal most of the time. In the fullness of time, I traced it to a worn generator pulley. It was the belt rubbing against the sides of the V-groove that was making the squeal.

The car was now fully functional, and I drove it to special occasions. The admissions director at the Hotel School was a particular friend of my wife. Her husband is a car buff, and they go to car shows in a considerable radius, as far away as Rochester and Hershey. There is a small local car show in Norwich, near Greene (southeast of Syracuse). Our friends talked me into entering the Armstrong Siddeley in this show. On the morning, we drove over in convoy, they in one of their stable, an unrestored 1926 Rolls limo. We followed a manure spreader up one of the long hills, which nearly reduced both of us to tears.

I was still having a lot of trouble with the transmission. There was nothing wrong with it, but I needed training in its use. Backing was particularly scary. The transmission tended to grab and jerk, shooting the car backward. I learned eventually to plant my left foot firmly on the brake when backing to provide a little control, and this worked very well. At the

The 1954 Armstrong Siddeley Sapphire 346 after the restoration.

time we parked at the show, however, I had not learned this yet, and I struck terror into the 1925 Cadillac behind me, who thought I might ram him and destroy his beautiful restoration. (I shared his concern.) At the show, my car attracted a lot of attention, and I was tremendously pleased to receive second prize in my class. My best friend and his wife were supportive enough to come to the show with a house guest to cheer me on.

Receiving the second prize (a truly hideous miniature gas pump on a wooden base) was heady stuff. Now, I wanted to enter the car in the big time — the Eastern Division Fall Meet of the Antique Automobile Club of America at Hershey, Pennsylvania. This is the world's largest regular automobile show, with perhaps 1800 cars on display, and attendance in the neighborhood of half a million people. It is held every year during the first week in October. The competition is intense, and only the very best cars are entered. My friends very delicately tried to save me from disappointment. They suggested that this was not the right approach — that one had to work one's way up to Hershey by entering first local, then regional shows, finding out what the judges did not like about the restoration, and correcting these things, slowly bringing the car up to the level expected at Hershey. I would not listen to reason.

In September of 1987, I registered the car for the show at Hershey. The

Back view of the 346. Four-lights (without the rear quarter-lights; see the Star, which has them) were very rare, and even rarer in this country. I believe this is one of 17 worldwide.

size of the show means that the arrangements are very bureaucratic. Each entrant is required to give extensive information about his car to determine in which category it should be placed. The organizers will not communicate with the entrant; he just shows up on the day and accepts whatever spot he has been assigned by the organizers. I can understand the reasons for this, but it is still annoying. I explained to the organizers that this car was one of only 17 thought to remain worldwide (11 in Australia, three in the US and three in the UK). I described the car inside and out. I suggested that it should be displayed in the category "Specified Prestige Vehicles 1946–1962."

The show at Hershey is so large that motel rooms have to be reserved a year in advance; a month before the date, no rooms are available within a 50 mile radius. I had to stay at Granny's Motel in Frackville, a tiny community about 50 miles north in a great wasteland off the highway to Hershey. I drove down the night before, parked the car in front of the entrance where it would be in the light, and went to bed. I was expected to be in line at Hershey at 7:00 in the morning. When I got up at 5:00, I shared the breakfast counter with a couple of deer hunters eager to be in the woods before first light.

As I approached Hershey, I passed increasing numbers of interesting old cars in beautiful condition. I began to wonder if I was being an idiot. The show is held in the parking lots of the football stadium. The line of cars waiting to take their position on the field is perhaps a mile long. Finally the entrant arrives at the organizers' table and is handed an envelope indicating in which category his car will be displayed. I had been placed in "Production 1946–1956," which I thought was insulting. This separated me from the Rolls-Royces and Jaguars and put me up against the Chevrolets and Fords. That may actually have worked in my favor, although I was asked all day long why the car was in this category. When I pulled up to my category, I was directed to park by a judge wearing roller blades, the better to get around the enormous area with some speed.

People who were interested in cars like mine did not expect to see such a car in this category, so they did not plan to visit this part of the field. Hershey is so large that some budgeting of time and energy is necessary. However, word got around, and friend told friend, so that after a while I had a gratifying number of visitors who had come by specifically to see the car. The judges eventually showed up, a team of four, each one specializing in a specific part of the car: inside, underneath, paint, and engine compartment, as I recall. Once they had left, I felt I could stop polishing and look at the other cars. My family was very supportive. My oldest girl, Katy, and her husband and two kids lived in State College, Pennsylvania, which is just a couple of hours from Hershey. They came down for the show, with a family friend. My wife had driven down the day before to spend the night with them, and she also arrived. Even my friend the car buff from Ithaca showed up. At the end of the day, it seemed to me unlikely that I had won anything. I tried to buttonhole a judge and ask if there was any way of determining whether I had won anything, so that I could decide whether to stay for the awards banquet, or to cut my losses and go home. I was exhausted from the early hour of rising and from trudging around Hershey all day. The judge was kind but firm, and revealed nothing. I figured my friends had been right, and I had overreached. We decided to leave.

Back in Ithaca, I had essentially forgotten the show when a letter arrived from the AACA in Hershey. The letter said that I had been awarded a second junior in my class but had not been present to accept the award. If I wanted it, I would have to send a packing and shipping fee, and they would mail it to me. I was ecstatic. The "junior" requires explanation: when a car appears for judging by the AACA for the first time, it is eligible only for a "junior" prize. When it has won a "junior" prize, it is eligible for a "senior" prize, and then for a "preservation" award. The prize was better looking than the previous one; this time it was a chrome-plated plastic loving cup, with a reproduction of a Duryea horseless carriage on top, the whole thing on a wooden base.

Going to car shows, and otherwise interacting with other enthusiasts, has been very interesting. Enthusiasts are for the most part very nice people, although many of us are a little tilted. Some enthusiasts are collectors, and never restore their cars. They talk of restoring them, but they never do. They may have barns full of semiderelict cars that make my palms itch to start fixing something, but all they do is wander among them and absorb the ambiance and perhaps stroke them. I really don't know — I can't join them when they are alone with their love, but it is clear that is what it is. Most of these collectors are outgoing people.

The other half are restorers. Many of these do not do their own work. They are very enthusiastic, and talk a wonderful game, but they buy everything done. Only a few do their own work. These range from mechanics or ex-mechanics on one end of the scale to complete amateurs with no experience, but a lot of enthusiasm, on the other end. I have only met a handful of other engineers. Among the real do-it-yourself experts are quite a few curmudgeons. I think cars attract more than a few who find they are more comfortable with machines than with people, just as engineering does.

In general, it is hard to find people who have solid, reliable knowledge combined with a cheerful, friendly personality. The breadth and depth of ignorance is shocking. Every now and then someone steps forward who clearly knows what he is talking about, but it is often from a historical or traditional, rather than rational, perspective, and sometimes it is marred by didacticism. We have this in academia, too — people who love being the experts. I have decided that I am happier restoring my cars than I am talking to other people about restoring the cars, with a few rare exceptions.

The next summer I found an excuse to attend National Day of the Armstrong Siddeley Owner's Club of Great Britain. The École Centrale de Lyon in France was awarding me an honorary degree. The timing was perfect, and on the way there Jane and I could stop at National Day.

National Day took place just outside London, at a stately home that had been turned into a sort of conference center. The cars were displayed on the extensive lawns, underneath the ancient trees. The weather was beautiful, something that cannot be relied on in England. These were the first functional Armstrong Siddeleys that I had seen, other than my own. Of course, they covered the entire production of Armstrong Siddeley, stretching back into the teens of the century, but there were a good number like my 346. *Schadenfreude* is not attractive, but I was delighted to find that the overall quality of the restorations was not very good. I also heard a number of comments about American restorations being "over the top," and being over-restored, which I interpreted as sour grapes. I took several rolls of film of relevant vehicles, but I could not find any evidence that I had done anything wrong in my restoration, except for the engine compartment. I had painted it in a red enamel from Rustoleum. It was not a professional thing to do, and I knew it at the time. It should have been in the body color. I don't know what got into me.

The members could not have been more cordial, and we were given a guided tour of nearly every car there, with a history of the restoration. Several families had brought caravans, or set up tents, and we had numerous invitations to tea. In the evening there was an informal dinner, followed by an auction of donated objects, some of them vaguely Armstrong Siddeley related. As the result of Jane's enthusiastic bidding, we ended up the proud owners of a curious arrangement — something like a basketball stuck through a hole in a circular board, so that the protruding part could be grasped between the feet. With a good sense of balance, one could bounce around the room. No Armstrong Siddeley connection, I am afraid. We carried it back across the Atlantic and still have it up in the attic.

Chapter 11

Jaguar

MOM DID NOT WANT TO go back to England when they retired. This was Dad's calculation, and it was basically financial. They had very little in the way of pension or health insurance. They needed somewhere that had a fully functional national health scheme and a relatively low cost of living. Dad offered Mom her choice of Devon or Mexico. She was even less enthusiastic about Mexico.

They needed a car, since they were not close to public transportation and were psychologically unfit to use it. Dad felt that he deserved a treat to compensate him for retirement, dislocation, reduction of income, and so forth. His solution was to buy a slightly used 3.4 liter Jaguar Mk. 2 sedan in pearl grey. This was a lovely car, and they used it regularly until he died at 87, some 20 years.

I managed to arrange professional trips to Europe about once a year and sometimes more often, stopping in London on one leg and taking the train down to Devon to see them.

The Jaguar was not very well maintained as it aged. My parents were short of cash, and body work is as expensive in Devon as anywhere else. Eventually, the front wings needed to be replaced, and considerable rust damage under the sills needed repair. Dad found a garage that would do a quick and dirty job involving pre-owned wings—just enough to get by the MOT (Ministry of Transport), the equivalent of state inspection.

Mom was also deteriorating slowly. It is not entirely clear what she had; it seemed like Alzheimer's disease in many respects, but not in others. Dad had his hands full, ferrying her back and forth to the hospital and to doctor appointments. My parents had made the right choice of venue to retire — Mom was dying on the National Health, just as they had planned, and it was not costing much. At this point, Mom often had no idea who I was. Several times after returning home we received calls from Dad, tiredly asking us to try to convince her that we had indeed been there, before turning the phone over to her.

I was on a professional trip to France when I got a call announcing that my father had died. Mom, of course, could not be left alone, so it was essential that someone get to Devon immediately. Jennifer, our middle child, was still in Belgium with Raymond. Jennifer and I got to Devon by the next morning. The woman who lived in the cottage across the street was coping, bless her soul.

With the help of a local lawyer, we managed to get Dad cremated, get Mom into a local nursing home, and get the house and contents sold.

I could not bear the thought of selling the Jaguar on the local market. The lawyer and I connived to have Mom (who would own it when Dad's will was probated) sell it to me. Her mind was still clear enough to understand this transaction on good days, like Hamlet, who could tell a hawk from a handsaw when the wind was southerly. We arranged to have the car shipped to the States. It had to wait while the will was probated, which seemed to take forever. During this time, it was stored outside, standing on earth, a very bad idea. Cars rust rapidly when stored this way.

The car was delivered to New York. It had been shipped in a container. I went down to collect it, to a terminal where containers were unpacked and goods reshipped. The place was run by a frenetically engaged young man, as active as a stockbroker on a trading floor. He was juggling several phones and directing the activities of several crews. My car had been unpacked, and it was determined that the fuel pump was not working. The place had a mechanic on call to repair their trucks, and they had put in a call for him to come and deal with the pump. This was clearly not a high priority. I could probably have increased the priority by offering a bribe — this was, after all, Mafia country — but it did not occur to me. I waited several hours for the mechanic, and then suggested in no uncertain terms that I go and get the pump and install it myself. They were a bit taken aback, but we located a dealer in the vicinity, and they sent me with a driver to pick up a pump. I had it installed in about 15 minutes, and then went to deal with the US Customs person.

I drove the car home to Ithaca, although it carried only a British registration. It was, of course, right-hand drive. I have driven right-hand drive cars on the left extensively in the UK and Australia, and left-hand drive cars on the left in the UK, but I had never driven a right-hand drive car on the right. It turned out not to be a problem except in a drive-through McDonald's, where I had a difficult time reaching the speaker to give my order. If I had looked under the car, I probably would never have taken it on the road. A great deal of rust damage had been done while it waited in England.

When I got it home and assessed the condition, I was appalled. Again the bottom six inches of the car were held together by paint. The previous repairs had been carelessly done, so that the rear door gaps had not been maintained, and the door closure was not correct. This was essentially irreparable. This is similar to the problem with the Spitfire convertible; both bodies are weak, but for slightly different reasons. If it is to be repaired, it has to be jacked up until the door gaps are correct, before the welding starts. This had not been done.

I got a lot of practice welding on this car. At about this time, on one of my trips to England, I was able to attend a national rally of the Armstrong Siddeley Owners' Club, which was held in Yorkshire. People could not have been more hospitable, finding me a place to stay and transporting me to the rally. In the evening, since it was known that I was doing my own work, I was introduced to two young men of frightening aspect. I remember earrings and purple hair standing up in spikes. However, they were tremendously helpful. They also were doing extensive restoration, involving a great deal of welding, and they introduced me to Stargon, a trade name for a mixture of carbon dioxide and argon. This single piece of information was an enormous help. At the same time, I obtained a board for the controller of my welder, which would turn the arc on and off at regular intervals. Finally, I bought a helmet that had glass that was transparent under normal circumstances but darkened automatically when exposed to bright light. This made a fantastic difference — now, for the first time, I could see what I was doing. When the first arc was struck, the glass darkened, and the instant the arc stopped, the glass cleared. I could always see where I was. The Stargon helped to prevent burn-through on thin material. Now, for the first time, I could successfully weld thin material and produce not only a strong weld, but a moderately good-looking one.

I must say that I did a very nice job on the body, but there was no hiding from the fact that this body was really too far gone to repair. This was not a keeper, as nostalgic as I was about the car. It was still a beautiful car, but it was a disaster waiting to happen. This was a car to put back together and sell, as rapidly as possible.

I did do a little to the interior. The dash had some damage to the veneer in the center. The veneer had come unstuck, probably due to sun damage, and a bit of the edging was missing. I delicately reattached the bit that was

Nice patina on the seats.

unstuck, and faked the edging, doing miniature woodgraining. Then I sprayed it with lacquer and rubbed it down. It looked wonderful.

The seats I refinished using Connolly dye and hide food. I also made new carpets and installed them.

I gave the car a quick coat of paint in pearl grey, approximately the original color. I must say that, when it was done, it looked very nice. I drove it for the better part of a year. I had done nothing to the engine, which ran very well but was tired.

At one point during the year, the brake servo failed. All it needed was seals, a few little synthetic rubber cups that seal the pistons in the servo. A seal kit for such a servo costs perhaps $2. I called England, attempting to find such a kit. I rapidly discovered that no one would sell me one because of the liability insurance. All that was available on the market was a rebuilt brake servo, for something in the neighborhood of $1,000. I suppose if I bought a seal kit and rebuilt my servo, and it failed, and as a result I ran down and killed a pregnant woman pushing a baby carriage, a suit might be brought against me and the kit manufacturer and the distributor.

I eventually found a sympathetic distributor who agreed to sell me a kit, so long as it was invoiced as a clutch slave-cylinder kit and not as a brake servo kit. They are of similar nature and similar price, and I happily agreed.

I finally needed the money I had invested in the Jaguar for another project. I tried to sell the car privately, and advertised it in a number of

Here it is, after my tender ministrations.

places. I got very few nibbles. Several people drove out and evidently thought they were in some sort of old car museum. They had a fine time looking at my cars, but were not serious about buying the Jaguar. A couple of serious people looked, but did not call back. I got one call from Japan, a very serious buyer. He was coming to the United States and would call me when he got here. He wanted a complete photo set. I immediately ran off a complete roll and rushed it to Wegman's, which had one-hour processing. When the pictures were ready, I sent them off by courier to his hotel room in Seattle. I never heard from him again. I finally decided to sell the car at auction. Jane was horrified, but I had been sponging on her for money to fund the restorations, and she had cut me off. I really had no choice.

It was time (the first week in October) for the fall auction at Carlisle, close to Hershey. I drove down. As it often does, it rained cats and dogs. The car performed beautifully, but the new floor leaked and the carpets on the driver's side were soaked by the time I got there. The cars are parked in a field for a morning, so that prospective buyers have an opportunity to look them over. The cars intending to cross the auction block are lined up, and the drivers stand outside their vehicles waiting for hours, if they are near the end of the line. Since I had not consigned beforehand, I was close to the end of the line. The Jaguar did not cross the block until sometime near six o'clock, as I recall. I had been hoping for something close to $10,000, which was approximately the book value for a Mk. 2 sedan in nice condition. However, I was rapidly disabused of this idea by the other owners in line. The received opinion was that to draw $10,000 the car would have to be "much crisper." I had thought it looked pretty nice, but I was certainly aware of its flaws. It was definitely not concours quality. I had set a reserve of $10,000, but when I approached the block I was asked if I wanted to lift the reserve. With my heart in my mouth, I did lift my reserve as the car crossed the block, and listened in disbelief as it was sold for $6,000. I was in shock. The seller before me, who had sold a nice E-type Jaguar, was also very upset at his price, and refused to honor the sale. He took his car and went home. We had all had to sign a form saying that we would not do that. I honored the sale, to a dealer in Rochester, with a terrible taste in my mouth. I was very angry, and felt that I had been robbed of probably $2,000, if I must be realistic. That was probably the dealer's profit — he would resell the car at retail for perhaps $8,000, what I might have been satisfied to receive. I collected my money and flew home. At least, the money received would cover my current costs.

Six months later, I received a call from a body shop. The Jaguar had been sold to a customer who had crashed it. The body shop wanted to know the paint code, so that they could complete the repairs.

Chapter 12

Armstrong Siddeley again

SHORTLY BEFORE I DROVE the Armstrong Siddeley down to Hershey for the show, I had seen an ad in *Hemmings Motor News*. It was for a 1960 Armstrong Siddeley Star Sapphire, the model following the first one I had restored, and the last one they had made. This car was in Newark. I called, and the person I spoke to suggested that I fly down. He agreed to have someone meet me at the Newark airport.

At the airport, I waited and waited; I called the number, and it seemed that there had been a misunderstanding about where I was to be picked up. Finally, a surly and uncommunicative guy showed up with a pickup truck. On the way, I tried to get a little more information. A part of me was beginning to wonder if I was being taken for a classic ride and would end up in cement overshoes. My destination turned out to be the Tri-State Toyota Distributorship, where Toyotas were received from overseas, and transshipped to dealers in New York, New Jersey and Connecticut. The owner of the Armstrong Siddeley appeared to be the supervisor of the distributorship. When I casually referred to him as Lou, my ride very seriously and carefully corrected me: "Louis." I was ushered into Louis' office with a certain formality, considering the utilitarian surroundings. I had the impression that Louis ran a tight ship. He was seated at a desk, in casual clothes. Behind him, leaning against the wall, was a serious man wearing a sports jacket. I was not introduced to him. I took the jacket to be a statement intended to set him off from the scurrying workers: "You work; I oversee." The whole situation felt like a B-movie, with Louis in the role of capo and the sidekick as enforcer.

The trailer with the bits and pieces.

Louis had the enforcer take me out to a back corner of the yard to show me the car. I could scarcely believe my eyes. The car had been stripped of all removable panels, doors, hood and trunk lid. These leaned against the wall in a trailer standing next to the car, which also contained a few cardboard boxes of assorted parts. The car was supported on concrete blocks and baulks of timber, because the rear springs had been cut off with a torch. The car had a vinyl roof; Armstrong Siddeley had never made a vinyl roof. The car was painted silver over blue, definitely not Armstrong Siddeley colors. What was left of the interior had been reupholstered in black vinyl. This had clearly been a pimp-mobile. The car was standing in the elements, so the woodwork was delaminating.

I took a few photographs of this sorry mess and went back inside to talk to Louis. It appeared that the restoration had been started by a friend, who got as far as dismantling everything. It then languished for some time, at which point the friend died. Before dying, he bequeathed it to a mutual friend. This friend made desultory efforts to continue the restoration, but decided that it was beyond his modest capabilities. Louis acquired it and temporarily parked it in the corner of the Tri-State yard, intending to complete the restoration. After it had rested quietly there for several years, a dele-

Barn fresh! Photographed in Louis' Tri-State yard.

gation came from Toyota to inspect the yard. They took one look at this derelict vehicle in the corner and without hesitation said "Out!"

The price was right. Louis was willing to give the car away to anyone who would take it. Even in its appalling condition, the distinctive lines of the car were evident. It still had an elegant roofline with a relatively low crown, creating an appearance of grace and elegance, almost fragility. I was a sucker; I bought it. I insisted on paying a nominal fee, feeling that some money should change hands to establish ownership, probably a silly idea without legal standing. Louis offered to provide transportation to Ithaca. A car transporter (belonging to the business) was heading north to transport Louis' brother's drag racer to a meet in upper New York state. The driver would call when he got near Ithaca.

I went home to wait for the call. Since Louis had to get the Star out of the yard fast, the wait would not be long. The day that I was going to leave to take the green 346, my first Armstrong Siddeley, to the big show at Hershey, I got the call. I agreed to meet the truck on the outskirts of town and lead him to my house. I was at the university. I went downstairs to the laboratories and collected four strong young men, and we went looking for the truck.

When the truck arrived at our house, a problem arose. The transmission of the Star was locked in drive, and could not be moved. This presented a problem. This was a Borg-Warner automatic transmission, which has a hill-holder. This is a freewheeling device that locks the driveshaft if the car tries to roll backward. The car had rolled forward to be loaded on the truck, but had to be rolled backward to be unloaded and, of course, the hill-holder prevented it from rolling.

The truck driver could not believe that the transmission could not be shifted, and tried by brute force to do so. He stopped just short of tearing off the shift lever. We all stood around scratching our heads for a few moments. Then the four strong young men started bouncing the car while pushing it down the ramp and off the truck. On each upward bounce, when the wheels nearly left the ramp surface, they could move it back a few inches. In this way, we managed to get the car down the ramp to the ground. However, we had been helped by the slope of the ramp, and we could not make further progress on the level ground.

We left the Star resting in front of the barn. I got back to the house, already considerably behind schedule for the trip to Hershey. It was beginning to snow. I ducked into the house to ask our cleaning woman to drag a piece of plastic over the Armstrong Siddeley and weight it down with stones. This was not exactly in her job description, but she did it with enthusiasm.

When I got back from Hershey, I had to get the Star into the barn somehow. I finally attached a come-along to the rear axle, hitched it to the posts supporting the barn, and started ratcheting. At each throw, I gained a few inches. I was worried about the barn, but it was strong enough.

At about this time I had a professional meeting in Dubrovnik, where I was to present a paper and possibly have a couple of good meals. I took the opportunity to stop at the UK Armstrong Siddeley Owner's Club's Northern Day, held in Yorkshire. There were a number of Stars like my new one, and I took several rolls of film of them, inside and out.

The organizer delivered me to the airport, and I flew off to Marseilles and Dubrovnik.

Back in Ithaca, once the car was inside the barn the first order of business was the engine. The car had been sitting in the yard in Newark without the hood in place, and the air cleaners had also been off. This had permitted water to enter the carburetors and also the cylinders that had open intake valves. Fortunately, this involved primarily one cylinder. Unfortunately, that cylinder had filled with water, which had run down past the rings and caused electrolytic corrosion between the aluminum piston and the cast iron cylinder wall. The piston was essentially welded in place.

I tried everything I could think of. First, all sorts of solvents and lubricants. None of these had any effect. Then, heat from an acetylene torch, as much as I dared. Nothing. Then, I chained the actuating cylinder of a four-ton hydraulic frame straightener to the block to push the piston out. I crouched well out of the line of fire, expecting something to fail catastrophically at any moment and fly across the room. To my amazement, nothing. I finally had to cut a large hole in the top of the piston and saw it into pieces like an impacted wisdom tooth. Amazingly, the cylinder walls were undamaged.

There was a worse problem, however. Close examination indicated that the block had been filled with plain water (without antifreeze) and had frozen solid at some point. There was a split along most of the length where the deck joined the manifold side. The deck is the machined surface on which the cylinder head fits. My heart sank when I saw this. When I was a kid, a cracked block was the kiss of death for an engine. People shook their heads sadly about the news of a cracked block, as over news of the unexpected death of a loved one.

At this point there are actually several options. One is to use the block as a boat anchor, and find another block. That is easier said than done in the United States, since the number of these cars that had been imported was very small, and none of them had been junked, according to the owners' club. Finding a block in the UK or Australia would have been fairly straightforward and inexpensive — the owners' clubs serve as clearinghouses. However, shipping a block to the US would have been expensive.

It is possible to repair a cracked block, although it is normally not economical. It is necessary to use welding rod of the same chemical composition, and raise the block to red heat and weld it at that temperature, letting it cool down slowly to relieve the stresses.

I located a man down on Long Island. Like many people in the old car hobby, he had developed a charming persona and a great line. He had spent his working life doing repairs like this in Argentina. He made his chemically correct welding rod out of discarded engine blocks. I gathered he had a pit dug in his back yard in which he built a fire to bring the block up to temperature, and when it was welded it was covered up again to slowly cool down.

I built a huge crate for the block, which probably weighed 500 pounds, and called for a truck to pick it up. When the truck arrived, I was given to understand that it was not the driver's job to load freight. With ingenuity and sweat and heavy planks I managed to get it nearly into the truck, and the driver grudgingly gave me a hand at the last minute. It was off to Long Island.

Nothing in this business happens quickly. I tried to be patient, but after a few weeks I started calling. These guys learn to tell charming, plausible stories to explain the delays, which are probably caused by overbooking or advancing age. My Argentinean connection had probably returned to the States at retirement age and was now in his mid-seventies. He probably undertook one of these projects only when he felt like it.

Finally, it was done. When a block has been heat treated like this one, it changes dimensions in every direction. Residual stresses that had been there since it was made relax. All the surfaces need to be remachined. My Argentinean connection sweet-talked me into sending it to a friend of his, who specialized in machining rare engines.

Both men did a beautiful job, and I was quite impressed with the welding, which was essentially invisible.

It was summer again, and time to start on the body. I removed the vinyl roof, to find that water had run down under it and pooled on the sides of the rear quarters, which were eaten right through. Of course, there was a row of holes across the roof, for the small sheet metal screws that held down the aluminum strip on the edge of the roof. I would have to think of a way of hiding those.

I decided to sandblast the entire car to remove as much of the rust as possible. I went through 600 pounds of sand before the car was clean. Fortunately, the floor of the barn was nice smooth new concrete, so that I could sweep up the sand and reuse it.

The rust had been very extensive. There were large and small patches of surface rust, as well as serious structural rust of the lower six inches or so of the body. I felt it was important to get something on the bare metal to protect it, no matter what repairs I was planning. I sprayed the car all over with a black polymer that seals rust permanently.

Eventually, I dragged the body around to the barn attached to the house, where I could do serious work. I detached the body and lifted it very carefully about a foot above the frame. It was very fragile, because so much of it had deteriorated. I removed all the parts from the frame and worked over it with a scraper, sanding disk, and wire brush; finished up with a sprayed solvent; and then painted it. This is something that I would not do for just anyone. In my barn, with no lift, it has to be done lying on my back on the floor, and all the muck scraped from the frame falls in my face and under my contact lenses, despite my face shield. The sensible way is to remove the frame entirely and sandblast it, or better yet, have someone else sandblast it. I have tried both, and the latter is certainly preferable.

Fortunately, the frame was sound, and none of it had to be replaced. It was also not distorted.

A new door-bottom. Note that the door skin has been pieced using a batten; not very professional, but it keeps it flat. Also note the new foot for the A-pillar, and the new sill.

On the nice, fresh frame I installed all the suspension components, which I had sandblasted, painted and re-bushed. I ordered a pair of used leaf springs for the rear from the owners' club in the UK and reconditioned them.

The body required extensive work. The bottom six inches of all the doors had to be replaced. The inner fender wells that formed the sides of the trunk were perforated, and had to be replaced. The whole trunk floor, with the well at the back that holds the tire tools, was rotted out. Fortunately, the owners' club in the UK had a new old stock replacement that had been waiting since the factory closed. I drilled out the old spot-welds and welded it in.

Between the Sapphire and the Star the factory had decided to get rid of the suicide doors and had moved the hinges to the front edge. This required that the rear of the front fenders be changed, to make room for the thick front part of the door when it swung open. A bulkhead was placed in the fender, perhaps six inches from the back, to make a pocket for the door. This created a mud trap inside the fender, and this whole section had rotted away. I had to fabricate the rear eight inches of the front fenders.

The new rear inner fender well and trunk floor. The upper level would have to be replaced.

When the new sections were welded in place, I used body solder to fair in the seams. This was the first time I had used body solder, and it was fun. Body solder predates plastic filler; it is a technology that goes back to the beginnings of the automobile industry. It is harder to apply, but it will last forever.

The heater-ventilator box (under the dash) always rusts out on these cars. Water can get in through the cowl ventilator and is supposed to leave through drains on each side of the bottom. These become plugged, however, and the whole box gradually fills up with rainwater. The firewall forms part of the back of the box, and that rusts through also. The owner's club in Australia recommends fabricating these boxes from copper flashing. On the 346 I used galvanized sheet, but here I used the copper and did a nice job, taking the copper up the back so that water could not contact the firewall.

The sills on this car were also rotted out, but this time rather than fabricate them I ordered reproduction sills from the owners' club. I also got new valances, which fit between the bumpers and the body. The owners' club had had fiberglass rear fenders made, and I got a pair of them.

Left: The rear of the right front fender. New bulkhead and new edge. A combination of pop rivets for clamping, and MIG plug welds. *Right:* The left front fender, faired in with body solder. Note that on this side the new section is even wider, and runs forward at the bottom.

The rear quarters, which had rusted under the vinyl top, I strengthened from the inside using Kevlar cloth and resin. I did not trust myself to beat new sections and weld them in without changing the contours in a visible way.

The section below the trunk lid, above the bumper, was rotted away, as were the front sections of the fender skirts and the lower front sections of the front fenders. For all of these I honed my panel-beating skills to form new sections, which I welded in.

I find it endlessly fascinating to acquire these antique manual skills. Of course, there is a learning curve for all of them. People used to earn a living applying these skills, and one can hardly expect to acquire them overnight. However, I was reasonably successful with these techniques. There were certainly things I might have done differently if I had had a second chance on some of these projects, but for the most part the first attempt was satisfactory. I was greatly helped by several small books written long ago by specialists. These little books are not literary masterpieces, but they are gold mines of information that can otherwise be obtained only by endless painful experience.

Here is my copper heater-ventilator box, with copper rivets and soldered seams.

Someone had stumbled into the hood as it leaned against the wall in the trailer, and it was buckled across the middle. I spent a long time with the patient strapped to a table, trying to find a way to apply enough force in the right direction to remove the buckle. I often wish I had apprenticed in an old-fashioned body shop; then perhaps I would know the answers to some of these questions. The most perplexing ones relate to how to grab some of these body parts so as to apply force to remove distortion, without doing more damage. It is a little like dealing with a greased pig.

The car had been black when it left the factory, with wide whitewall tires (gangster whites, as they are called), and I had decided to restore it to that state. This is very dangerous; black shows up imperfections terribly. Old car people say that if it is perfect, paint it black. At car shows, you see people like me crouched down sighting along flat panels, looking for telltale ripples. There were certainly a few that could be spotted that way, but not many.

The condition of the wood was appalling, since it had been exposed to the weather for a long time. The dash was delaminating. I managed to relaminate it; I also repaired the other woodwork, since many of the pieces had splits and cracks.

The new sills on the right side.

Whereas the Sapphire had had no veneer on the cant rail (above the side windows), the windscreen surround or several other places, the Star, since it was trying to be the poor man's Rolls-Royce, had veneer virtually everywhere. I got a batch of veneer, but it was not nearly as nice as the veneer I had gotten for the Sapphire. I was told that this was due to the fact that Jaguar and other manufacturers were beginning to use walnut veneer again (after years of using plastic and photo-reproductions) because of the availability of tougher modern finishes. This new demand had sucked up all the good veneer. The veneer I got was not flat, and I had to spray it with a glycerin and water solution and put it in a press to flatten it.

A contractor friend offered me some catalyzed varnish used for kitchen cabinets. I used this to finish the veneer, and it did a lovely job. On the exposed edges of the plywood, the factory had used an opaque tinted varnish, so I tinted the finish I was using and sprayed the edges with it.

At about this time I had an opportunity to visit Coventry. There was a meeting at Warwick, which is quite close by, and I took a day off and visited the Rolls-Royce Heritage Trust, which is just across from the num-

Provisional fitting of the rear section. My cute panel-beaten section welded and leaded in behind the bumper. Note the new trunk floor.

ber three gate of what used to be the Armstrong Siddeley main works, the Parkside Works. It is the Rolls-Royce Heritage Trust because Armstrong Siddeley Motors, after having been bought by Bristol to become Bristol Siddeley Motors, was bought by Rolls-Royce; both buyers were interested in the aircraft engine business, and took the car out of production. The primary purpose of my visit was to view a Star Sapphire maintained by the trust; I hoped this would be in more nearly original condition than any I had so far been able to view. Sadly, while much of the exterior was original, the carpets (my particular interest at the moment) had been replaced, and so could not be trusted for originality. The trust is staffed with retirees from the works, and we had tea and a nice chat about the Armstrong Siddeley Sapphire jet engine that I had tested at Curtiss-Wright.

Back in Ithaca, I still hadn't decided what to do about the carpets. For their edging, the factory had used something called coach lace. This is a fabric tape, woven in a subtle same-color Jacquard pattern. Something like this is obtainable commercially, but it is much too wide. I couldn't find anything suitable. Chris' wife, Melissa, is a weaver and knitter by trade, weaving blankets and scarves and knitting sweaters. For Christmas that year, I

The reveneered dash, door cappings and windscreen surround. New upholstery and door panels.

received a curious small package, which I opened while Chris and Melissa were exchanging knowing looks. It was a roll of coach lace of the right width. Melissa had woven by hand yards and yards and yards of this complicated narrow patterned stuff. I was overwhelmed. Of course the original had probably been made on an automatic Jacquard loom controlled by punch cards, while Melissa had no mechanical aids. It looked beautiful, and just right on the carpet.

I did the upholstery, which is more complex than that of the Sapphire. On each seat cushion and back there is a central pleated panel in a raised surround. The surround is formed by a molded foam piece. These had all perished, and when I removed the covers, the foam fell apart. Faced with the prospect of making new ones, I went out and bought foam at the local Woolworth. By experimenting, I discovered that foam can be smoothed by a sanding disk, the kind used to grind sheet metal. It is necessary to use a light touch, and the foam has to be restrained so that it will not fly across the room, but the sanding disk is quite controllable so that nice, gentle curves can be produced. I had to form the surrounds for four seat cushions and four seat backs, so it took a while. The welting between the raised

The trunk, with Melissa's coach lace just visible around the gas filler. The suit-case is my father's old one from the period (and it has a French Line tag on it). It contains oil, coolant, spare radiator hoses and other emergency supplies.

surround and the pleated panel is restrained to the back of the seat by string, so that it will be depressed and stay that way. The upholstery looked very nice in red, the original color.

It was time for the chrome, always a source of anxiety. A considerable fraction of the chrome for this car was simply missing. The car had been dismantled and pieces put in cardboard boxes, and had then sat in various garages and back lots and been moved several times. It is hardly surprising that here and there a box had been mislaid, or left behind in one of the moves. However, with the exception of a very few items, the chrome was one thing that the owners' club in the UK could not help me with. I contacted the owners' clubs in Australia and New Zealand. From the club in New Zealand, I heard of a Star that was beyond restoration and was available for parts. This was a singular opportunity — so far as the other owners' clubs knew, no Star had ever been parted out or junked, although several had disappeared from the records.

I called the owner and we negotiated a reasonable price. There was to be a conference in Australia, and I arranged to attend. I would be able to stop over in New Zealand and collect the chrome from the car and bring it home with me. I told the owner roughly when I would be there.

The delay was not very long from an academic point of view. In academia we normally plan our lives a year ahead, roughly. To agree to attend a conference, prepare a paper, submit it to the organizers, and so forth, takes about that long. As I recall, in this case the delay was only a few months.

When I landed in New Zealand I was staggering with fatigue. I had been to Australia twice before, and the trip to New Zealand is nearly as bad; it is a nightmare. The flight goes on forever, even now when it can be done nonstop from San Francisco to Christchurch (it used to stop in Hawaii and Papaete). I recall being brought to attention by the posted weight of the plane at takeoff, which was more than half fuel. The captain stopped just before leaving the gate, to have the tanks topped up again after the foam had subsided. That made me wonder just how much reserve we had against unforeseen contingencies. My friend Zellman (from Melbourne) says that there is time to get drunk, sober up, and get drunk and sober up again before arriving.

New Zealand strikes me as something like Canada squared. It makes me long for the old Times Square. It is so clean and neat and orderly and buttoned up — it puts me in mind of Quaker communities and religious resorts on the Jersey shore. It is physically beautiful, and the people are warm and generous, but I do wonder why the children don't all leave to find somewhere more lively.

I had two things to do. First, I had arranged with the owners' club to view a Star that was in good, unrestored condition. It had recently been bought by Penn Bradly (resident in Canberra, Australia), for export to Australia. However, Australian law places a much lower tariff on the import of a car that has been owned for more than a year, so Penn was storing it with a friend in New Zealand for a year and a day before importing it. It was a lovely car, in superb condition, and someone from the owners' club drove me around in it for a while and took a picture of me and the car. All this passed in a fog of jet lag.

Then, I had to prepare myself to collect the chrome. I would need shipping containers. I went to a garden supply place, and bought lengths of PVC pipe with pipe caps to contain the longer pieces. I had made measurements before leaving home of what I would need. I went to the back door of a discount furniture store and begged a discarded cardboard carton. I took this back to my hotel room and fabricated a container of the right size for the rear window surround, using the utility knife and tape that I had bought locally.

From the time of my arrival, I had been calling the owner hourly to arrange to collect the car, but there was no answer. I had made sure before coming that he knew exactly when I would be there, so I was perplexed. This was getting critical — I had a strict timetable that I was obligated to stick to. I called the secretary of the owners' club to see if he could help. He said he would make some calls and get back to me. Within the hour, he called me back with the news that the owner had sold the car to someone else, and was not answering the phone because he didn't want to talk to me. I was speechless with disbelief.

Fortunately, the secretary of the owners' club got the name and address of the new owner. He was on the North Island, but I could go there fairly easily. I called him, and we discussed the possibility of my buying the chrome. He tentatively agreed to sell it to me and said some other things that I did not understand, between my jet lag and his accent. I arranged to go up there to see the car, as I thought. The secretary of the owners' club drove me to the airport, and warned me that this person was known to the club; evidently he used to be a member, but was asked to leave because of some shady transaction. The secretary was trying to be so discreet that just what had happened was not clear.

I flew up to the North Island, carrying my PVC pipe and cardboard boxes. When the new owner met me at the airport, he looked perplexed at the pipe and box; I explained what they were for. He looked at me as though I were an idiot, and asked if I hadn't understood that the car was not there, but still on the South Island, awaiting shipment? My heart sank. This trip was not turning out well.

The new owner looked a bit frightening; but perhaps this was the influence of the information I had just been given about him. He was about 45 years old and looked like a man who would rather use his fists than argue. His farm was run down and did not seem to produce anything. However, the man was extremely hospitable. He had several other Armstrong Siddeleys, and a few other interesting cars in various states of disrepair, scattered about in the numerous sheds and barns. We had an interesting day. We had lunch with his wife and daughter, who both had a demeanor that suggested to my fevered imagination that they were regularly beaten. There was also a dog who gave the same impression.

After lunch, he proudly showed me a collection of new old stock parts he had obtained with another Star. When the first owner had bought the car, he had also bought a stock of parts sufficient to maintain the car in the middle of New Zealand. In the event, the car had not needed the parts, and here they were. Among the parts were two factory seal kits for the Borg-Warner automatic transmission, still in their factory wrappings. I wanted one of those seal kits so badly I could taste it. I had not done anything to my transmission so far; without a seal kit, there wasn't much I could do. Even though the car was all together, I could still remove the transmission and rebuild it, if I could get one of those seal kits.

I am not an experienced, or delicate, negotiator — I tend to blurt out what I want and pray that the other guy will take pity on me. However, this time I found reserves I did not know I had. I spent the entire afternoon carefully laying the ground, dropping an occasional remark. By the time we left for the airport, we had negotiated a price for the chrome, and I had left my pipe and box with him, with written instructions as to just which parts I needed and how they were to be packed. However, the seal kit was still not a done deal. He took the kit with him to the airport, so I felt that there was a good possibility. However, we were still discussing the matter when I got out of the car. It was not just a matter of price; he wasn't sure he wanted to sell the kit at all. Or, that was his negotiating tactic. The final deal was made over the top of the car, with him on one side and me on the other; when they called the flight he handed over the seal kit and I handed over the money and ran for the plane.

Despite the disturbing aspects of this whole operation, after I returned to the States the chrome showed up on time, all correct and accounted for. The disturbing aspects were probably all in my imagination, induced by jet lag.

Meanwhile, the trip was not finished yet. I flew on to Australia, to Canberra, where I was scheduled to give a talk on restoration techniques to the ACT branch of the Armstrong Siddeley car club. Penn Bradly put me up at his house. He and the car club could not have been more cordial, holding a banquet in my honor and taking me out for a barbeque (they really do say "barbi," as in "Put another shrimp on the barbi!"). Penn drove me around town in his Hurricane, the first postwar Armstrong Siddeley model, a convertible. When we went out for the barbeque, he rolled out his Siddeley Special. This is an enormous custom vehicle from about 1936, of some eight liters displacement, a chauffeur-driven limousine with a division. When I left, the car club gave me a framed copy of a Star Sapphire advertisement.

Now, I had to go to Melbourne to sing for my supper — present the paper that justified the entire trip. All the Australian airlines were on strike, and the government, in an attempt to break the strike, had brought in the Australian Air Force to transport passengers. I had the pleasure of flying to Melbourne in a huge C141 Globemaster cargo plane, the kind that can swallow several tanks up a tail ramp. We sat in seats like cargo nets, in four long lines parallel to the fuselage, under the command of the loadmaster.

Sadly, on the return trip, the strike had been settled and I flew on a normal commercial plane.

When I returned to Ithaca bearing the transmission seals, I looked in the phone book for a transmission repair shop that could deal with a Borg-Warner automatic transmission. I had rebuilt quite a few transmissions, but never an automatic, and I thought it would probably be a good idea to find someone who had. In fact, there was someone in Ithaca who advertised that he understood Borg-Warner transmissions. This is probably because Ithaca is the home of Borg-Warner. The transmission is the same one that Jaguar used in the same time period.

When I took the transmission in to the one-man shop, together with the seal kit and the manual, it became clear that the proprietor was not the expert on these transmissions that his advertisement suggested. It seemed that the expert had actually been his father. However, he assured me that he felt competent to deal with it, and if he ran into trouble, he could always ask his dad, who was still around and *compos mentis* but did not come into work because of his knee replacements. I worry that this is how many mechanics, including me, will end up.

I waited a considerable time before calling. He assured me that it was coming right along, but was not quite done yet. I waited some more. When I called again, it was evident that nothing was happening. He was stuck, or had run out of steam, and was giving his attention to more profitable jobs that did not present a problem. I offered to suit up and go over to give him a hand putting it back together, and he accepted. We needed several gaskets, which had to be made. He did not have punches for doing this, being accustomed to having kits of all the gaskets required. I went home and made the gaskets.

We got it all back together and I took it home. He was nervous about letting it out of the shop without being able to road test it, but I assured him I would bring it back when the car was all together. I installed it and found immediately that it did not function correctly. It was not shifting into high gear. I made all the tests that were recommended by the manual, measuring the pressure in the various circuits. Some of the pressures were not right. Before removing the transmission and tearing it apart, I felt that I should get some advice from someone who knew what he was doing, and I did not feel that this was our friend from the shop. The UK owners' club put me in touch with the man who had designed the transmission, now long retired. I called him at home, and he very kindly walked me through the whole thing. He asked me about the pressures I had measured, and he identified the malfunctions that could be responsible. His analysis agreed with mine, which pleased me. There were two possibilities, one complicated to fix and one simple. I thought it was probably the simple one. I removed the transmission and checked. It was as suspected: a gasket that had not had a hole punched in the correct place; I am happy to say that this was not one of the gaskets I had made, but one of the last ones that our friend had made before he gave up. With the gasket corrected, the transmission functioned perfectly.

When the chrome arrived, it was necessary to prepare it for the plater. None of it was in very good condition. This time I was using a plating place in the deep South. Before sending off the pieces, I put tape on each section that had been filled with silver solder and wrote on the tape with magic marker FILLED WITH STA-BRITE. When I got the pieces back I found that the marked tape had been completely ignored, and the filled pieces had all been buffed before being plated. This is what I was trying to avoid. The buffing removes a lot of the soft Sta-brite, so that the surfaces that I had carefully flattened were no longer flat. When plated, this is evident: instead of being mirror-like, the surface is distorted, like a fun-house mirror. I did not have the stomach to redo everything and send it all back — it represented an enormous amount of my work. I decided that the window frames were adequate. The pieces that had not been filled were fine. The long strips below the doors I did send back to be redone, carefully explaining what I wanted. They made the same mistake again. I decided I could live with it; I could not bear the anguish of doing it a third time.

The car was finally done, and it was beautiful. Despite the slightly wavy panels here and there, the overall impression was really very nice.

I got a small oriental rug that just fitted the floor in the back seat. I have been told that these little test patterns are made by Pakistani girls to demonstrate that they have mastered the skills necessary to make full-sized rugs.

Now it was time to go to Hershey again. This time I started well in advance, and sent the Antique Automobile Club of America lots of supportive material, including a copy of Penn Bradly's new book on the postwar Armstrong Siddeley cars. I wanted to be placed in the class that included Rolls-Royce and Bentley, and other elegant cars. It worked.

Jane and I drove down together. As usual, the weather was appalling. It usually rains at this time of year (the first week in October), but this time it outdid itself. It poured. At night, with the windshield wipers on high, I couldn't see the edges of the road. The interstate was closed, and we were reduced to feeling our way along country roads, trying to find Granny's Motel. In the morning it cleared, we breakfasted at 5:00 with the deer hunters again, and lined up to get into the grounds at Hershey at 7:00. When we had parked on the field, we began giving the car a final polishing.

Top: No waves visible here. *Bottom:* Nice rear line. You would never know it was a fiberglass rear fender.

Here we are on the field at Hershey. Left to right, Audrey, Mark, Katy, Jane, me, Jonathan and the Star. Mark is an old friend of Katy and Robert.

I discovered that enormous amounts of rainwater had entered the trunk during the drive down. The factory had decided to fully carpet the trunk, just like the inside of the car, and the carpet and underlayment were soaking. This could probably be traced to an accident that the car had had when it was new, detailed in the factory file. It had been rear-ended in Hackensack, and the owners had written the factory to get a replacement trunk lid, which was a less than perfect fit. Fortunately, the carpet looked normal — only if it was touched was the squishiness evident.

Again, I had no idea how we had done. There was a complication this year: the timing of the show was awkward for me, because I had to be at a scientific meeting in Poitiers, France, immediately following the show. I had to leave directly from the show, flying to New York and on to Paris, and leave Jane to bring the car back to Ithaca.

When I returned to Ithaca, I found waiting a message from the Antique Automobile Club of America saying that I had again won a Second Junior, and that if I wanted my trophy I should send some money to cover shipping and handling. I was delighted, but I was beginning to get annoyed. Professionally I have never been satisfied with second best, and I did not like it much in this venue, although it was certainly better than no prize at all. Unfortunately, the judges will not share with the contestants the details of the judging; it is not possible to determine what was not right so that it could be corrected the next time. I determined to do an even better job on the next car.

I drove the car on a number of trips; once up to Vermont to visit Chris and Melissa, and once to a consulting job in Canada on the eastern shore of Lake Huron. It is a wonderful car to drive, comfortable and responsive. During the summer, I drive it around Ithaca, and back and forth to the university.

The Star had been finished and taken to Hershey in 1991. In 1996 we were driving down to State College, Pennsylvania, to visit Katy (our oldest) and her family. Perhaps 20 miles outside Ithaca, we came to a crossroads known as Alpine Junction, distinguished by a gas station and a bar. There is a light at the junction. We were probably going about 60 mph. As we approached the junction going south, a car going north began to turn left across our path. The car had started its turn too late, and there was not time; still, if it had moved quickly, it could have gotten out of our way. It moved at a snail's pace. Other northbound traffic was approaching in the outer lane so that I could not go around the car to my left. I stood on the brakes, which are excellent, with vacuum-servoed disks on the front. The pavement was dry, and no one could have stopped faster. However, it was impossible. Our speed was down to perhaps ten mph when the Armstrong Siddeley hit the other car just in front of the passenger door.

No one was injured, but my beautiful car was severely damaged. The bumper, grill and right front fender were a mess. Neither car was drivable. While we waited for the police we disconsolately retrieved bits and pieces of the car from the pavement.

The driver of the other car was an 80-year-old woman who was known locally as a menace on the road. The local position was that she was fine on the back roads, but should not be allowed on the main roads. After the accident, her sons talked her into giving up her license.

The Armstrong Siddeley was taken home on a roll-back by a very sympathetic man. We used the roll-back winch to pull out the fender enough to permit the car to be steered. He cut the fan belts with his pocket knife, so that the engine could be run for a few minutes to back the car into the barn.

We contacted the other driver's insurance company, and they sent an estimator to look at the car. I was still seething about the accident and was not very cordial. However, he was also very sympathetic, and accepted the price list that I had gotten from the owners' club in the UK for the parts that would be needed. In addition, he gave me generous figures for my time

The new dumb irons welded in place.

to do the repairs; generous, at least, for commercial body work, though they would not compensate me for the extra time required for a show car.

Unfortunately, the Armstrong Siddeley would have to wait two years for its repairs, until the winter of 1999. When the accident happened I had already embarked on my next project, and since I have only one bed in my intensive care ward, there was nowhere I could work on the Armstrong Siddeley.

When I was finally able, I started on what are called the dumb irons. These are the extensions of the frame that carry the bumpers. They are made a little lighter so that they will crumple in an accident, and they had. I cut them off where they joined the stiffer frame and made new ones, which I welded in place.

A very expensive fender sent from England, which would have greatly simplified the repair work, could not be made to fit. It was a repaired fender, and the angles of the patches were not correct and no amount of body solder could fix the problem.

I put the crumpled fender back on, then screwed into the headlight opening a piece of heavy plywood with a large screw-eye in the middle of it, and hitched it to a tree with a come-along. I tied the rear axle to the posts of the barn with wire rope. This did a pretty good job of pulling out

The fender, straightened out as much as possible.

the accordion folds in the fender, and I was able to remove most of the remainder with a hammer and dolly. It was pretty good, but not perfect.

Fortunately the collision had missed the hood, which had popped open and slid right over the other car — it was undamaged.

The car is now restored to a respectable condition, and I am again driving it every day. I can see the residual traces of the accident, but I doubt that anyone else would see them. It is still a very satisfactory car and a pleasure to drive. I am afraid that in the aftermath of the accident my attitude toward driving has completely changed. I now approach situations which contain the potential for that type of accident with my heart in my mouth, expecting someone to do something disastrous. The feeling is slowly going away, but I suspect it will never go away completely.

Chapter 13

Lagonda

THE STAR WAS DONE, and I was at a loose end. I was filling time reupholstering some of our furniture.

At the same time, I had my eyes open for another car. I read everything I could lay my hands on that might help — I devoured ads in *Hemmings Motor News* and in the back of all the British car magazines I receive. I was pretty well committed to another British car. Having done several, I knew how the Brits did things, and knew the names of reliable suppliers for all the bits and pieces I would need. I didn't want to go back down to the bottom of the learning curve and start again on another country.

I saw a couple of ads for 2.6 liter Lagonda convertibles, with pictures. I thought this was a very interesting-looking car, and I read up on it.

After W.O. Bentley's company went bankrupt around 1930 and was bought by Rolls-Royce to form the new Bentley Motors Ltd. in 1931, for a while Bentley stayed on at Rolls-Royce as a sort of advisor. Everyone found this very uncomfortable; they did not really need or want him, and he knew it, but it was part of the deal when they bought the company. In 1936 the Lagonda company also went bankrupt, and the receivers proposed bringing in W.O. Bentley as technical director. He leaped at the chance and designed several very sophisticated and attractive cars before the war. Bentley was convinced that British laws would change and that after the war it would no longer be possible for wealthy people to own large, expensive automobiles. During the war he worked on the design of a smaller, less powerful car, which he felt would be perfectly positioned in the market at the end of the war. This was the 2.6 liter.

The war finally ended, and Lagonda struggled in the face of steel shortages to bring the 2.6 liter to market. Bentley felt that having his name on the car would help sales considerably. He wanted to call it the "Lagonda Bentley." Unfortunately, Rolls-Royce had bought the exclusive use of his name when they bought his defunct company. When they heard through the grapevine what he had in mind, they threatened suit. Bentley went over and talked to them; he agreed not to use the Bentley name, and they agreed to withdraw the suit. When Bentley got back to Lagonda, the managing director was so incensed that Bentley had caved in (as he saw it) that he called Rolls-Royce and told them to do their worst, that Lagonda was going to call the car the Lagonda Bentley. Of course Rolls-Royce sued, and won, and the settlement bankrupted Lagonda for the second time.

A new actor then came on the stage: David Brown. Brown had made a considerable fortune manufacturing tractors and transmissions. Now he wanted to have a little fun. He had just bought Aston Martin (also bankrupt) and was planning to design a lightweight car that would be competitive in racing. He was interested in Lagonda because of the very nice engine that Bentley had designed for the 2.6 liter Lagonda. This was a double overhead cam, six cylinder engine with a barrel crankcase. Brown bought Lagonda and used the Bentley 2.6 liter engine in his new space-framed Aston Martin, and this became the DB2 (for David Brown), which was very successful in racing. He brought Bentley's Lagonda to market with very few changes, substituting a gearbox of his own manufacture for the Coatal box that had been planned. The 2.6 liter Lagonda was manufactured from 1947 to 1951. It was expanded to 3.0 liters and the body redesigned in the 1951–1953 period.

However, the traditional Lagonda people in the owners' club have disowned this car (and the 3.0 liter), primarily because it was manufactured by a tractor manufacturer. It is not considered a *real* Lagonda. As a result, the price is substantially lower than that of any other Lagonda.

The more I read about this car, the more attractive it looked. It was like an undervalued stock. It was mechanically and historically interesting, pretty, and yet relatively cheap.

I joined the Lagonda Club and began reading the ads in its newsletter. These cars are not numerous. Only 250 were made, including sedans and convertibles. Perhaps 50 convertibles were made. They do not come on the market very often. Eventually, I did see an ad in the newsletter. I called the owner and talked to him about the condition of the car. The owner took some photographs of the car and sent them to me. It was really cute.

I wanted to go and see the car, and probably buy it, but it was complicated. The car was in a place called Rumbling Bridge, north of Edinburgh.

I was supposed to give an invited talk at the École Polytechnique at Palaiseau, just outside Paris. I would probably be able to arrange my flights so that I passed through Edinburgh. I called and made arrangements with the owner.

After the meeting, I flew to Edinburgh. The owner of the Lagonda met me at the airport. He was an English architect working in Scotland. We arranged that I would spend the rest of the afternoon sightseeing in Edinburgh, then I would return to his office and we would go to his home together.

The architect drove me home. He lived in the country in a large house, probably from the early part of the century, with outbuildings and a great deal of land. I was to stay with him that night and the next, and go home the following day. I would be able to view the Lagonda the next morning. In the afternoon, he had made arrangements for me to visit a restoration facility in a small village a bit farther north, where his other 2.6 liter Lagonda convertible was being restored.

I was a little suspicious that what was being offered to me was a parts car, perhaps used as a donor for his own restoration project. However, he showed me bills indicating that a great deal had been done to this car: a lot of welding on the chassis, and a great deal of wood replacement in the body. Although it might have served as a donor, "parts car" seemed an exaggeration.

The following morning he went off to work and left me to look at this car and at the rest of his collection. He had five or six cars of various sorts. The Lagonda was incomplete, as the convertible top and windshield had been removed, but I was assured later that they would accompany the car. It was very difficult to get a clear view of the underside without a lift, or a jack and stands, or a light, but it was evident that there had been a lot of welding underneath, and that this was of very poor quality and would mostly have to be redone. I managed to find a battery that was not flat, and attached it and determined that the engine was free. The fuel pump was not working, however, and I did not have the strength to take it apart and find out why. The upholstery was in amazingly good condition. The body was also in remarkable condition. It was a handmade aluminum body, so rust was not a problem. It had been given a quick coat of paint — without proper surface preparation — which would certainly have to come off. (The owner told me that evening that it just needed a couple more coats and a polish, and it would be lovely.) Without dismantling the car, it was impossible to tell much about the quality of the wood replacement, although I could discern a few pieces that had been replaced (in the trunk and under the dash), and they appeared to have been competently done.

The Lagonda in Scotland.

After lunch, the owner had made arrangements for me to use one of his modern cars, an undistinguished little station wagon, to drive to the restoration facility. This turned out to be a going concern, employing at least half a dozen men doing panel beating, mechanical work and trimming. Their paint spraying was done locally by another firm. I met the proprietor, a nice, and clearly competent, man. I saw a number of interesting cars there: several large Rolls-Royces from the early thirties, and an E-type Jaguar among others. The work they were doing was of the highest quality. The proprietor's daughter did the upholstery, and did a lovely job. They had a large room in which were stored many cars under restoration. These restorations had been stopped because the owner of each had a temporary cash flow problem. The proprietor was indiscreet enough to let slip that the owner of my Lagonda had a number of restoration projects at the facility, but that they were all currently on hold. I concluded that my owner had a cash flow problem also, which he was hoping to partly resolve by selling the Lagonda that I was examining. I saw my owner's personal Lagonda 2.6 liter convertible, which they had pulled out of storage for me to look at. Just before putting it on hold, they had been welding up fatigue cracks in the aluminum body, which seemed to be everywhere. This seemed a bit ominous. The welding was beautifully done, and I had a long talk with the man doing it, whose burr was so thick I almost needed a translator.

That evening, after dinner, we began negotiating. *Thoroughbred and Classic Cars* has a listing each month of the market value of old British cars in four states of repair, from excellent to a restoration project. This was definitely in the latter category, since it was not running and did not have an MOT (equivalent to a state inspection sticker). Unfortunately, we had both seen this listing — he had a copy of the magazine next to his chair, and I had one in my briefcase. As I recall, £7,000 was what *TCC* suggested for a restoration project. His position was that the car was much better than that — look at all the work he had had done. Why, to bring the car up to concours standards would require hardly any work. When I pointed out the poor quality of some of the work he had had done on the car, he suggested that I was a typical American, having an exaggerated concept of concours quality, producing "over the top" restorations. At one point his wife chimed in, asking him if he had checked with his daughter (away at school), since she had always been very fond of this car; she would be devastated to learn that it was being sold. The picture was that the car had been a beloved family vehicle, used for many fun outings during her childhood. I doubted it very much, but it was possible. Certainly, any such use was not recent.

He had started at £10,000, which corresponded to the next category up from the bottom. After an hour or so, we were down to £9,000, and it didn't seem that we were going to go any farther. He kept saying that if he could not get that figure for it, he would have to think about what else he might do with it. I suspected that he needed £9,000 for some purpose (to pay a creditor?), and so could not settle for less. I felt that I had the choice between abandoning this vehicle, returning to the States empty handed to look for another, and paying this price. I should have tried throwing in the sponge, to see what the effect would have been. However, I really thought the car was cute, and would have hated to abandon it. He could probably sense that. I finally agreed to his price. His son had been there for dinner. Even he got into the act, asking his dad if he was really going to let the car go that cheaply.

Of course, I did not have enough ready cash to buy this car, but I could come up with about half of it, and he agreed to wait a little while for the other half.

He got out all the paperwork he had accumulated on the car; a photocopy of the owner's manual and of the parts list, and all the bills. It was nice to have something I could touch. I was beginning to feel a little of the pride of new ownership of something exciting, but it was an uphill struggle so far from home, with the prospect of probably half a year's wait before I could lay hands on the car, and the whole thing somewhat soured by the knowledge that I had paid too much, due to a combination of incompetence at negotiating and greed. Besides, I was not entirely comfortable with this guy, who I suspected (with no evidence whatever) might be involved in several shady deals. The quality of the welding bothered me; had he paid good money for this work, and never looked underneath to check it? Or, had he checked the work, and thought it was fine? Or, had he quietly negotiated for a quick and dirty job to sell the car? Anyway, I didn't feel I could trust what he said. I also didn't believe the son and daughter stories, which I thought were produced for effect. In fact, his whole pitch about the condition of the car was disturbing; did he believe it? Did he think I believed it?

However, it is only fair to say that I liked his house, which was filled with interesting old things—every step of the stairs had a bit of memorabilia. Of course, that could have been his wife. I also liked his car collection. I suppose there is nothing inconsistent about a man with good taste and possibly questionable standards, any more than it is inconsistent to have a president who had questionable standards in some respects but was good at foreign policy and politics.

In the morning he drove me over to the Glasgow airport for my flight home.

On my arrival, I immediately began scraping together all the cash I could lay my hands on. I have various royalty checks and honoraria that come in from time to time, and I jealously hoarded these. Fortunately, the first quarter of the year is a good time for this. Within a few months I had accumulated the difference, and sent it to the owner. Then we began the arrangements for shipping. He was going to see that the car got to the docks and on the boat, which was very convenient for me. He obtained a firm price, and I sent him the amount.

The car was shipped, and I eagerly awaited its arrival. Finally, I received notification that it had arrived. However, I was informed that it was not being released, because the shipping charges had not been paid. Dire threats were made of storage charges mounting up daily. I called the number of the former owner and got no answer. I had several other numbers, including his work number, and I called that. I was coolly informed that the owner and his wife had left for an extended sailing vacation in the Mediterranean. At the time I had to make a trip to the West Coast. Imagine me and a colleague waiting for delayed flights in crowded airports, with incomprehensible public address systems blaring constantly, with me at a pay phone, one ear plugged, yelling at somebody in Scotland as I tried to get the situation untangled. At one point I was talking to the man in the shipping office in Edinburgh, who, it transpired, was an old friend of the former owner; I asked him why, under the circumstances, he would impound the car for nonpayment of shipping charges? There was a moment's silence, and then he muttered that that was the way everybody did business. I think the answer probably was that that was the only way to be sure of getting his money.

Eventually, one of the messages that I had been leaving got to the former owner in the Mediterranean, and he paid the shipping charges (saying that he had forgotten to leave word in his office to issue a check). As quickly as the situation had arisen, it was resolved.

Now a new situation arose. The terminal in New York began sending me bills for various inexplicable things. With each one, I was assured that this was the complete and final bill. Then another bill would arrive, for some charge that had not been included on the previous bill. They all had a certain plausibility. I was sure I was being taken to the cleaners. Some of the charges were demonstrably incorrect, and I complained, and they were changed. They denied that they had knowledge of facts I had stated on various forms. Threatening faxes from writers of English as a second language flew back and forth: "[Company] Inc. has been rejected [sic] your check and forwarded back to your home address. Please forward..." "Please advise your customer ... ALL PERSONAL CHECKS MUST BE CERTIFIED!" In order to get a straight accounting, I had to have my lawyer call them. This produced an itemized bill, complete with errors of over 400 dollars. I finally paid, so that they would release the car. However, I did not intend to let the matter drop.

I complained to the Interstate Commerce Commission, and their involvement got an immediate response. Now I received concerned phone calls and letters from highly placed executives apologizing for not replying earlier, thanking me for pointing out errors, apologizing for them, and enclosing checks for the difference. By my estimate of the amount they overcharged me, we had approximately split the difference.

This vehicle was way beyond my modest financial means. Initially I had considered only the price, which was already steep, but which I could just manage. However, it was becoming clear that there were going to be other costs that would be very substantial.

Now another problem arose. The car was delivered on a roll-back (the delivery price included in the astronomical fee). As the driver rolled it down the ramp, it was evident that there was something seriously wrong with the right rear suspension that had not been a problem when the car was shipped. The suspension was now collapsed, so that the bumper on that side hit the ground when the car reached the bottom of the ramp, and it was difficult to get it off the ramp and onto the floor. When questioned about this, the driver was inarticulate and noncommunicative, and essentially denied all knowledge of the matter.

The driver had a form that I was required to sign, indicating whether any damage had occurred. I indicated the problems I could see before signing. When the driver had left, I crawled around under the car to see what was going on. It was evident that the container had been dropped in unloading, landing on the right rear corner and collapsing the suspension. In addition, the left front fender had a serious crack just above the internal support, also probably due to excessive loading from the drop.

I filled out the requisite report for the insurance company and sent it in. After a long wait I received a wonderful letter that stated in part: "It has been noted by insurers that the car was 'very dirty' and 'scratched and chipped all over' ... and it was noted ... that the 'car is old and in poor condition.' In view of the above, it is with deep regret therefore that I inform you that it is the decision of the Insurers to deny liability for the damage to your motor vehicle as there would appear to be no evidence to suggest that the damage occurred during insured transit and therefore no grounds for the claim. Please be advised that I can be of no further assistance in this matter and that my file is now closed."

The high-handed tone of this letter incensed me. I sent them a fax pointing out that this was not just an old car, but a collector's car, and giving the market value in restored condition. I pointed out that I was an acknowledged expert in the field and had served as an expert witness, so that my word should carry some weight. However, I am sure none of this had the slightest effect. The stroke of genius that I am sure did have some effect was to fax copies of all this to the lawyer in Devon who was handling my parents' estate, indicating on a fax to the insurance company that I was doing so. The lawyer was a bit perplexed to receive all this, but since he was not required to do anything, he played along.

I thought there would be no response, but after more than a month, I received a letter asking for more information: how had the car been packed, how had the torsion bar come unsprung? This was a good sign (the file was reopened), but it also indicated that they had given the matter no thought or attention. I wrote them a long letter detailing exactly what I thought had happened, and precisely what evidence had led me to this conclusion, in words that could be understood by an idiot, with copies to my US lawyer and the British lawyer.

Eventually, they asked for estimates of the cost to repair the damage, which I sent. They finally paid what I asked. This was only a little over $300. I should have asked for more; in particular, compensation for the emotional distress brought about by the necessity of dealing with them.

Getting the car had been in every respect traumatic, but a little exciting. And very expensive. Now it was time to get serious. I removed the body

The rotted-out front cross member with the boxing-in removed.

completely, and removed the drivetrain, suspension and brakes, and everything else on the frame. Then I dragged the frame out into the driveway and treated it with a rented pressure-washer in an effort to remove 50 years of grunge.

Now that the frame was more or less clean, it was apparent that there were severe rust problems. The frame had been made up from relatively thin sections spot-welded together. Presumably this had been done because it was a fabrication technique that did not require heavy machinery. It is also possible that it had some connection with steel shortages following the war — perhaps certain forms and thicknesses were not available.

This technique had a serious disadvantage in that the space between the thin sections formed pockets that could hold water. The front frame cross member as originally designed had been too flexible. To stiffen it, it had been boxed in. This created a water trap. Progressive rusting from this trap into the pockets between the sections had destroyed the front third of the frame. Since rust occupies about eight times the volume of the original metal, the frame rails looked like a boa constrictor that had swallowed a pig.

In addition, the front engine mount carriers were rusted away, and the bonded rubber mounts themselves had totally perished.

The new cross member, before being boxed in. Note the new frame rail in the background. The upper A-arm towers and shock absorber mounts are just visible at the top.

My heart was in my mouth, but I didn't see any alternative — I would have to make a new frame for the front three feet. I would have to make a new cross member and engine mount carriers in any event, and the front sections of the frame rails were, in fact, easier to make. The most nerve-wracking thing about this reconstruction was the wheel alignment. The caster of the front wheels was entirely controlled by the geometry of the attachments to the frame; no adjustment was provided. Caster largely determines the tendency of the wheels to be self-centering — to want to return to the straight-ahead position if the steering wheel is released. If I didn't get this right, the car would be undrivable. I was also concerned about my welding; we didn't want the frame to fall apart after a couple of thousand miles.

The fabrication of the new front frame cross member was a delicate operation, since it involved the location of the lower A-arm pivots. These were critical to wheel alignment.

The towers that carried the upper A-arm pivots were next. I laid out their positions on the top surface of the frame according to the drawings in the owners' manual and welded them in place. My fate was sealed: either things were in the right place or not, but short of cutting everything apart, there was no way to change them. I would not find out until the car was back together, which would be a long time later.

I fabricated the various engine mount carriers and welded them in place, and also placed all the other carriers (for the rack-and-pinion steering, for example) back in place.

Now the frame had to be sand-blasted and painted. I built a little room out of 2" × 3" wood and polyethylene sheet. Inside the enclosure, we had a serious sandstorm. Visibility was almost nonexistent. I was wearing a breathing mask and a sandblasting hood, and with a high-intensity light I could barely see what I was doing. I had to stop periodically and shovel the sand back into the hopper.

At this point, real life intruded. My wife had very serious health problems, which made major changes in our lives, at least for a time. For me, it might have gone two ways. I might have stopped working on old cars completely. Instead, I desperately needed something to take my mind off these problems. When you have done everything that can be done, and there is nothing to do but wait, worrying and agonizing is not productive. I found myself working on the Lagonda even more. It was impossible not to remind myself how unimportant restoring old cars is. However, the work has its own ethic. Even in distress, I couldn't bear to do an unprofessional job. There is also the phenomenon well known to emotionally disturbed patients: when faced with a situation that you are powerless to alter, it gives some satisfaction to fix something that is within your control, even if unrelated.

Eventually, the frame was clean and I painted it. Assembling the suspension components did not pose any problems, with the exception of the little rubber booties that keep dirt out of the ball joints. After a diligent search, I concluded that these were genuinely no longer available. Rubber parts are always a problem, because they have a finite shelf life. Usually some organization like an owners' club will reproduce them. In this case, however, since only 250 of these vehicles had been manufactured, it had evidently not been worth anyone's trouble to do this. Ordinarily I can count on at least one of anything to still exist somewhere — it is only a matter of finding it. I have a few contacts that I call who can usually find odd things like a discontinued headlight gasket. In this case, however, I struck out.

I sought the advice of John Pinner, who is in charge of sourcing and fabricating parts for the UK Armstrong Siddeley Owners' Club. He was for many years an engineer in an automobile company. I had had extensive contact with John in connection with the extrusion of weatherstripping for

The new cross member has been boxed in. Note left-hand side steering and engine mount, upper A-arm pivot and shock absorber mount.

these cars. He suggested that I make the kind of dust boots that are used on prototype vehicles, before rubber boots have been manufactured. These are constructed by cutting out rings of leather and stacking them up, sewing the inner edges of the first and second rings together, and the outer edges of the second and third together, then the inner edges of the third and fourth, and so on, making a little accordion-pleated tube. The end pieces must be the right size to fit over the machined surfaces on either side of the ball joint, where they are wired in place. These looked very nice and have worked perfectly.

I was able to obtain many of the rubber parts that were needed for the suspension and the engine. The engine mounts were one problem — I could not find anything suitable anywhere. These mounts consist of a slab of rubber bonded to two steel plates to form a sandwich. Each plate carries bolts by which the mount is attached. In desperation, I had a number of these plates cut out and drilled, and I welded in the bolts. I made a deal with one of the big rubber molding companies, and they turned the plates into mounts. However, their minimum order was for far more mounts than I needed. Through the owners' club, I placed an ad for mounts, and finally got replies from half a dozen people. I sold off the surplus mounts and paid off the molding company.

The bushings for the rear torsion bars were another problem. They were very special, and nothing like them was available. They had been made by Metalastic originally. John Pinner put me in touch with a long-retired engineer who had worked for Metalastic. I called him up, and he was delighted to talk about these things and tell war stories. With his help I successfully fabricated the bushings.

Getting parts was not as easy as it had been for the Armstrong Siddeley. Aston Services Dorset had bought up the factory stock of parts when the company folded, and would have been an excellent source. However, they had an agreement with Aston Services Needles, in Needles, California. Any customer in the United States had to place his order with Needles, which would transmit it to Dorset, where it would be filled, and sent to Needles, and on to the customer. Of course, a fee was added to pay Needles for its time. I did not object to that, but I did object to the delay. However, Needles proved to be intelligent and sympathetic, and the system worked very well for a while.

One day, when I called Needles, a strange voice answered. Over the course of several phone calls, answered by different persons each time, I found out what was going on. The proprietor, who had been so intelligent and helpful, had been charged with statutory rape for what was claimed had been consensual sex with a 16-year-old. This last I heard from a very indiscreet woman who answered one day and clearly enjoyed gossiping. The proprietor was convicted and jailed, where he stayed until long after my restoration was completed. The replacements were a disaster — phones weren't answered, parts didn't arrive.

In the meantime, Dorset was having its own problems. Old Colonel Foreshaw, who had started the operation, was getting on in years. The business was essentially turned over to his two sons, who were not spring chickens either. They ran it very well. Unfortunately, however, the son who had the primary responsibility dropped dead one day, and the other son was so devastated that he felt he could not continue. When last heard from, the business was up for sale.

Fortunately, I had obtained the majority of the parts that I could not live without before either of these disasters struck.

The shop manual says that the cylinder liners should be seated in goose grease to seal them. I could have gotten goose grease, by the simple expedient of cooking a goose and collecting the grease (which would have had the collateral benefit of a good meal), but I also had a copy of the factory record, which indicated that early in its life, the car had been back to the

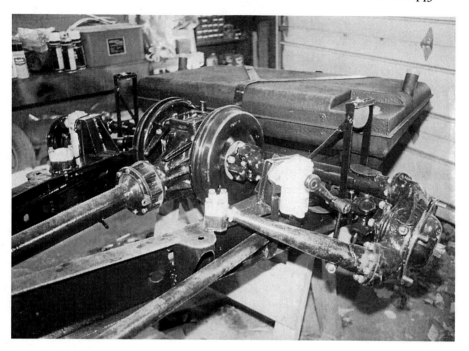

The rear suspension after restoration. Note W.O. Bentley's inboard rear brake drums, lever shocks, and ball joints for forward A-arms. The torsion bars run just inside the frame rails. A glint of light is just visible from the top of the right one, just below and forward of the ball joint.

factory twice to have the liners reseated. This suggested that goose grease might not be the best choice for a sealant. I decided to replace the goose grease with silicone sealant, and I liberally buttered the liner gaskets with this before dropping everything into place.

I took the cylinder head down to Cramer's for reconditioning. Cramer's was a general automotive parts place with a machine shop. They left something to be desired in the way of quality but made up for it in friendliness. I was allowed to hunt for things back in the stacks, the sort of freedom I had had in Detroit. They gave the occasional professional discount. Lou Cramer, who had started the business and had been an astute businessman, had long since retired, although he would show up from time to time on Saturday mornings to discuss his health with any customer who would listen. Lou's bills of sale were wonderful — utterly illegible. They might have been written in Aramaic. The business had been taken over by his son, Mark, who was full of wonderful schemes but had very little business sense. One day he wanted to restore the Ithaca streetcar line (his uncle, a scrap dealer, had taken up the tracks when it was discontinued); another, he had submitted a bid on antique rolling stock and was going to have a spur and a shed constructed so that the old engine could be brought to Ithaca and restored. He was going to set up satellite distributorships in surrounding communities. He was going to establish an engine reconditioning business. He was going to organize some of the NOS parts that his father had never sold and sell them over the Internet. The one thing that he couldn't do was slowly, steadily expand the business and be satisfied with the limited profits available there. To be fair, it is a tough business, and getting tougher. Fewer and fewer people work on their own cars, and there are more and more places like Joe, the Motorist's Friend, who cater to what I think of as nonserious mechanics who just want to change their oil. To afford to carry serious parts and maintain a machine shop, a place has to service a large area, much larger than Ithaca.

Mark's machinist was a relatively young and not very experienced kid. He made a subtle mistake in reconditioning the head that would, under normal circumstances, have been terminal. When Mark Cramer gave me the news he looked like someone announcing the death of a friend. Fortunately, we thought of a clever way to save the head by breaking all the rules; I went in and, working all afternoon, we brought it back from the dead.

When the chassis was back together, it was time to start on the body. The body was made of relatively small aluminum panels tacked to a hardwood frame. This frame, in turn, was supported by what is called the body tub, a sheet steel skeleton that carries the structural load of the body and passengers.

When the body is constructed, the factory starts with the body tub, which is welded up on a jig. Then the various wooden parts are bolted to the tub until it begins to look like a car. Then the panels are tacked to the wood, until it is a car.

I discovered that the repairs that had been made were even worse than I had thought. The individual repairs were very badly done, but in addition the tub had not been made into a load-bearing unit. This left the wood of the body to carry the structural load. Much of this wood had been replaced and was in good condition, but matters could not be left this way.

I slowly started reconstructing the body tub. By the time I was finished, I had replaced some 80 percent of it. Both side beams again had had lightening holes in the inner faces, and no drains, and so had completely rotted away. The repairs were a joke, and were not worth trying to save. The rear seat pan had accumulated water when the car was left out in the rain with the top down, had rotted through, and the water had run down

The finished engine, back in the chassis. The wiring is temporary.

into the crossbeam in back, which had rotted out. All of this had to be replaced. The floor in the trunk had disappeared long ago and had been replaced by a piece of plywood. There was enough left of the supporting pieces around the edges that it was possible to tell how the floor had been made.

When the body tub was sound again, I reunited the body and the frame. It was time to have the old paint removed from the body before I started to work on it. I located a place in Syracuse that did media blasting. This is like sandblasting, but uses ground up plastic instead, which is kinder to the surface. The place I found did furniture refinishing, and used media blasting to remove the old finish.

I called for a roll-back, but there was a delay before it came. Time was getting very short before closing time, and we had a wild ride to Syracuse. I followed in my pickup, my heart in my mouth, as I watched the roll-back careening around the curves, expecting my precious Lagonda to slide off at any moment. Fortunately, it was tied down securely. I had the various removable panels in the back of the pickup. We made it to the furniture factory just before closing and got everything unloaded.

Beginning on the body, I had to deal first with the doors. These sagged appallingly. They had wooden frames, and the joints at the corners were no

Repairs to the body tub. This is the left-side beam, which is all new. Note the gusset on the end of the crossbeam at the rear. The "rafters" that support the floor are original. Eventually a new floor will be placed over them.

longer rigid. All the joints had to be reinforced. A lot of the wood in the doors had been replaced, but here and there they had missed some rotten wood, which had to be stabilized.

The hinges were in terrible shape: they had been attached with wood screws. The screws had pulled out, and various attempts had been made to fill the holes and tighten the screws. They were also not in the right place. Making a proper job of the doors, getting them to close properly with a satisfying thunk, taking the sag out and fixing the hinges so they would last forever, took days for each door.

By the time I was finished with the body, I would have a lot of experience with the filling of old screw holes and their relocation. I started with a red oak floorboard, and by the time the body was finished it looked like Swiss cheese—I had cut probably 300 end grain plugs from it and glued them in.

The aluminum had fatigue cracks everywhere. If aluminum is properly supported it does not develop fatigue cracks. However, if something gives way because of a design flaw, so that a part is not properly supported, then the cracks start. As soon as a section begins to deflect excessively because of a propagating fatigue crack, this causes cracks elsewhere. It is a progressive disease. I spent a lot of time welding the fatigue cracks, and making supports to strengthen sections that had not been properly designed at the factory.

Over the course of 50 years, the convertible top had probably been replaced at least ten times. Around the back of the passenger compartment the top was attached by tacks to a strip of hardwood. This had a sort of stubble all over the surface where the top had been attached. The stubble was made up of the remains of nearly a thousand tacks that had lost their heads. It was easy enough to replace these wood strips with fresh ones. However, on the rear quarters, the tacks had been driven into the wood through the aluminum bodywork. This was as intended. However, the aluminum looked like

A closer look at the joint between the rear cross member and the left-side beam. The wheel well serves as part of the end of the crossbeam and also serves in part to transfer the load between the crossbeam and the side beam. Note the gussets to strengthen the side beam in torsion where the door post is attached.

Münster cheese after all this time. Although this would be covered by the top and no one would ever see it, I couldn't stand knowing it was there, so I cut out the offending sections and welded in new ones.

The body tub and body took the better part of two years to finish. By the time it was ready for paint, I was more than ready myself — it is hard to sustain enthusiasm without some gratification. The car had been a sort of maroon when I bought it. I had my heart set on a deep scarlet or garnet. Some of the cars of the royal household in England are finished in a color

The left side of the new trunk floor. The left-side gas filler pipe will go through the hole. That side panel stays put when the floor is removed to get at the rear brakes.

scheme of a garnet body and black fenders that I think looks wonderful. I got out my VW sunroof to spray test panels and bought some likely colors. Alas, I found that as I darkened a red, it turned brown. I was incapable of producing a dark red. Presumably this is because the reds I was mixing with had too much yellow. I should probably have used a pure mixing color rather than starting with a commercial dark red. However, I abandoned the process.

Mark Cramer was going out of business. As a last act of kindness, before he auctioned off the contents of his store he bequeathed to me his color books. He had been a distributor of R&M paints, although he didn't have trained, experienced personnel to mix the colors. With the color books in hand, I picked out the darkest, most saturated red I could find, a Chrysler color as it happened.

The media blasting had caused a certain amount of warping of the surfaces, and fixing this required a judicious application of filler. I used a thin filler called Icing, which is white; the hardener is red, and when mixed the filler is pink, looks just like icing for a child's birthday cake, and has the consistency of heavy cream. It spreads very nicely in a thin layer and can then be sanded to remove the waves.

The convertible top frame. I spent most of a winter getting this aligned properly both up and down, taking the rattles out of it with spring washers and making new brass plates to cover the end grain.

Approaching the final state, I wet a rag and smeared it over the surface to make it temporarily glossy, to pick up the reflections. When painted and polished to a high gloss, every imperfection will be evident, usually long waves; only by making the surface glossy can you see these waves. I was delighted to read recently that Pininfarina panel beaters, making handmade Ferrari bodies, would take the panels outside in the sun and smear oil on them to see the long waves that had to be removed.

It was time to paint the Lagonda. It is such a rush to apply color. After all the laborious surface preparation, in the twinkling of an eye the filled and primed sow's ear is transformed into a silk purse. If you have not been careful in the surface preparation, this is when you will pay the price. It is a crushing disappointment to look at a painted fender and see that there are ripples (which you thought you had removed) that will have to be consciously ignored; to realize that you have produced yet another ten-foot paint job, and to realize that correction is now impossible, that it is much too late. This only needs to happen a couple of times to make you extremely compulsive. Fortunately, the Lagonda looked lovely nearly everywhere. There

The body with its beautiful coat of paint. The rear fenders were painted while loosely attached to the car. The front fenders and nose piece were painted separately (one of them is in the background under the masking).

were a couple of small problem areas that were not as good as they might have been, but they were in locations where they were not too visible. The work does not need to be uniformly ideal, as long as the parts that are less than perfect are in locations to which the eye is not led. And, of course, the imperfections must not be very great.

I don't know whether the convertible top and frame that were delivered with the car had ever been on this particular car or not. In any event, they did not fit. The shape of the car had changed after the wood had been replaced; that would probably have been enough to keep the top and frame from fitting. Or, these might have been from the other car I had seen in the restoration facility.

I was missing what the Brits call the pram irons—the Landau joints (like an elongated S on either side on the rear quarter), which guide the top when it is unfolded and lock it into place. I had been promised these when I bought the car, and I had written dozens of letters to the seller in Rumbling Bridge begging for the pram irons. He never answered. I knew that the restoration facility that I had visited had a set of pram irons (on the seller's other car), and that they had access to a casting facility. I got in touch with them, and they were delighted to make me a pair, cast using the ones that they had as patterns. When my pram irons arrived they were perfect, and not inordinately expensive.

I spent the better part of a winter fitting the top frame to the body, making new wooden sections and tightening up all the joints, so that the top would be symmetrical and would open and close correctly. I went to considerable trouble to locate two cars like mine (the only two I could find at the time), one on the south coast of England near Bournemouth, as I recall, and the other just outside Lyons in France. Both were owned by Englishmen. The man near Bournemouth was happy to provide me with photographs of his convertible top inside and out, and delivered them in short order. The man in France was more elusive; he simply didn't answer his mail.

Fortunately, I had a longstanding relation with the École Centrale de Lyon, one of France's best engineering schools. I had established and for many years been the coordinator of a graduate exchange program between Cornell and the ECL. Several of the faculty at the school were old professional colleagues. By e-mail I raised my opposite number at the school, Mlle. Lambreche, a bilingual young woman with a degree in medieval French from an American university. She began bugging the owner in Lyons, calling him at random times until she connected, and then sweet-talked him. In fairly short order I received a roll of film from him, with pictures of his convertible top inside and out. God bless Mlle. Lambreche.

I had never made a convertible top before. I selected an acrylic material, two layers of canvas sandwiching a piece of rubber. It was a lovely oatmeal color. This was not the original type of material, but it would last a lot longer.

The first difficulty was how to deal with the vast expanse of material, as heavy as a tarpaulin. I finally moved the sewing machine out to the middle of the room and built a plywood table around it. However, I found that the large areas of canvas would not slide on the plywood. I taped polyethylene sheet all over the table, but that still was not enough. Finally, I sprinkled cornmeal on the polyethylene, and that did the trick.

The binding on the edges added three thicknesses of canvas to the single thickness of the top. When this had to make a square corner it was quite impossible to fold a sort of hospital corner (like the corner of a well-made bed, or the corner of an expertly wrapped Christmas package), since this would have added another three layers. This material was very thick and did not take to being folded gladly; six layers was quite out of the question. I had to learn how to clip the parts that would be hidden when the binding was stitched, so that the binding would lie flat.

The other problem area was the rear quarters. These are stretched in two directions, and it is essential that they be ripple-free to look right. Although ripples do not affect the functionality of the top, they scream "Amateur!" There is essentially no leeway in how these are cut: if they are not cut properly, there is no way to remove the ripples by stretching. Considering that I had no pattern and had never made a top before, I did pretty well. One side is virtually perfect, but the other is a little slack. It does not ripple, and it looks better or worse depending on the humidity and how the sun catches it. If there is ever a next time, I can do better. The trouble with this business is that I am often doing things for the first time and seldom get a chance to try again.

The front corners also presented a slight problem, because it was not clear how these should be folded. However, the top that came with the car, that did not fit, had at least been folded correctly, and I could take it apart and see how it should be done. At about this time, the Great American Race passed through Ithaca, and I was asked to display one of my cars. I took the green 346 down, and while I was waiting I inspected the tops of all the many convertible entrants. This was very instructive, and also gave me a realistic idea of standards in this craft. Although we have all seen many convertible tops, I assure you we do not look at them with real care until we have to make one from scratch.

For a finishing touch, I went down to our local dealer in oriental rugs and found a nice little one that would fit in the back. The front presented greater difficulties. I finally settled on two small Turkish flat-weave rugs about 16 inches square. These look very nice.

The upholstery was in remarkably good condition, with a couple of exceptions. The wooden panels for the doors had been wet so often that they were falling apart. The attachments that had been intended to hold the door panels flat on the door frame had rusted away, and in an attempt to keep the panels on the doors, they had been nailed in place through the leather. In the rear seat, the seat back was built on a piece of plywood. The lower edge of this sat in the seat pan, which had been filled with water frequently when the car was left in the rain with the top down. There was not much left of the plywood, although the upholstery was in good condition. In both these cases I was able to remove the leather, make new wood, and glue and staple the leather to the new wood.

This left the problem of the nail holes that had been made in the door panels. Fortunately, there is something called crack filler. This is a wonderful material that can be smoothed into a crack or hole in leather, and when dry can be sanded. If it is then sprayed with the right dye color, the mend is invisible. Since I was going to recolor all the leather, I used the crack filler to fill the nail holes and various other problems.

The interior (without front seats). The upholstery and wood is done, and the carpeting.

Connelly hides of this period were not vat dyed, but were essentially painted. What was put on is referred to as dye but is really a type of lacquer. Old, worn leather can be recolored fairly easily. My leather came out looking very nice.

I was browsing the Internet one day when I came across a site for someone in Switzerland advertising a Lagonda just like mine. I was stunned; considering the extraordinary rarity of the car, I had been happily thinking of myself as the only person in the world restoring one of these. I should have known better. The site had lots of pictures of various parts of the car to show how nicely restored they had been. I could click on each picture to enlarge it, so that I could examine the details; the parts did look very nice. The whole car was photographed in an alpine meadow with wild flowers. No matter how carefully I looked for imperfections, the car seemed lovely. Of course, it was difficult to see just what the upholstery was, or how good the paint job was.

I had to see this car in the flesh. In the sciences, meetings are being held constantly all over the world. If you want to visit Brazil or Kuala Lumpur it is only necessary to watch your mail carefully for a month or two, and you will find an invitation to a legitimate scientific meeting somewhere reasonably close by, or at the very worst so located that Kuala Lumpur is on the way there or back. This is probably what Senator Proxmire has suspected for years. Of course, you have to pay for this privilege by writing and presenting a paper at the meeting. However, we are all writing papers fairly continuously; all that is necessary is to pick the next paper in the pipeline that is more or less appropriate to the subject of the meeting, and do a little judicious rewriting to make it fit a bit better.

Happily, in a month or so I was invited to a nice meeting in the Italian section of Switzerland, organized by the Swiss Federal Institute of Technology in Zürich. It was to be held at Monte Verita (the Mountain of Truth), now a conference center, but renowned during the twenties as a hotbed of free love, theosophy, vegetarianism and communism.

I contacted the owner of the car and made arrangements to meet him in Zürich to view it. I was presuming it would not have been sold by then, since this was all several months in the future. Everything moves pretty slowly in academia.

When the conference was over, I caught the short flight to Zürich. I checked into my small commercial hotel shortly before dinnertime. The young man who owned the Lagonda picked me up in it a few minutes later. The car really did make quite a splash in the setting sunlight, next to the flowers in the hotel forecourt. A pretty woman came up and asked what kind of car it was. We drove with the top down for a couple of miles to the garage where the owner had done the restoration. This was in one end of a deserted warehouse. Waiting there was the man who had helped him. He had been sent by central casting to play the part of the kindly old Swiss grandfather; say, Heidi's grandfather with a moustache rather than a beard. The two of them could not have been nicer; the young man spoke a halting English, and the older man none at all, but they put the car up on the lift, and we examined every part of it.

It was a fully functional car that had clearly been in much better condition than mine at the beginning of the process. It was clear that Heidi's grandfather was a superb mechanic and had helped the young man sort out the car mechanically. Cosmetically, however, I felt many mistakes had been made. The interior trim was not original; carpets and upholstery were not correct. The paint job was of poor quality and not a believable period color. A number of parts had been chromed that should not have been. The refinishing of the wood was not as it should have been. I don't like to indulge in *schadenfreude*, but I certainly did feel a certain relief that this was not serious competition for mine.

After the viewing, we all went out for a pizza at a local pizzeria. I had brought a book of pictures of my car, and they were suitably impressed.

After dinner, we said goodnight to grandfather and the young man took me back to my hotel in the Lagonda, still with the top down.

Back in the States, it was again time for the big show at Hershey. This time, there was no problem with recognition of the Lagonda by the AACA. It was placed in the group with sports cars of the period. Driving down to Granny's Motel it poured, as it had done every year. There was drifting fog and heavy traffic. Twice the highway was closed because of a multiple collision induced by the fog, and I was forced to go off on the tiny side roads. The windscreen wipers would work for a while, and then quit abruptly. I have still not sorted that out. It was terrifying moving along at 70, sandwiched between two 18-wheelers in drifting fog and generally poor visibility, with unreliable wipers and brakes that were appallingly bad. I had relined the front brakes with modern brake lining, but they did very little to stop the car.

Fortunately, we got to Hershey without incident, and the rain stopped on the day of the show. Our good friends Shelly and Tonie came down for the show, having met me at Granny's. Katy and Jonathan also came down. The Lagonda excited a lot of comment. I was still polishing it when a man came up, saying that he had just finished restoring one exactly like it, and did I have any brakes? I explained my problems, and he said that he was a professional mechanic and told me what he had done, to no avail whatever. I was happy to learn that he had made a number of bad decisions in his restoration, so he was no competition.

When the judges show up, they come in a team. One judge is assigned to the engine compartment, one to the underside, one to the inside, and one to the paint. There is a head judge to coordinate the group. As I waited nervously, the head judge sidled up to me and spoke quietly. My imagination was running wild. What he said was: "Is it fun to drive?" I lied and said "Yeah!"

Later that afternoon, a judge came over and asked if he could look at the car. I was perplexed; the judging was over. In any event, why would a judge need to ask if he could look at the car? Seeing my perplexity, he explained that when they saw the list of entries, he had wanted to be assigned to the team that would judge my car; but he had been assigned to another team at the last minute and would now like to see the car in detail. I gave him the grand tour, and he was very admiring.

When it came time to leave, the Lagonda would not start. How humiliating! I have a booster pack, something like a lightweight battery for situations like this, but it had never occurred to me to bring it. People were leaving the field as rapidly as possible, anxious to get home after a long day. I was afraid I was going to be left all alone in the middle of the huge

The finished car just before going to Hershey. Note the hubcaps, which were very difficult to mask for painting. This is the better side of the convertible top.

field, with no way to get myself and the car home. Fortunately I found someone who took pity on me — they knew someone who had a booster pack, and we got the Lagonda started. Old car people are generally very kind and helpful.

The Lagonda has two six volt batteries in series, to produce 12 volts. One battery is on each side of the engine compartment, connected by cables running under the dash. I had bought period batteries. They are modern batteries inside, of course, but they are in cases from the period so that they look correct. They looked lovely, but quality control is not as stringent on products like this as it is on normal commercial batteries. One of the batteries had a dead cell, despite their being brand new. I managed to get home without a problem, although I was in a panic when I had to turn on the headlights later that evening.

Partway home, but before dark, I was cruising along when I vaguely noticed an 18-wheeler passing me. But he didn't pass. He was hanging just on my left front quarter, neither speeding up nor slowing down. "What in the hell is he up to?" I thought. Then I noticed that the driver's companion was turned around, squatting on the seat cushion, holding a camera and trying to get a good shot of the front of the Lagonda. He waved when he had gotten his shot.

When I left Hershey, of course, I did not know if I had won anything. You have to stay for the evening and attend the banquet for that. We know how I feel about things like that, even if they are car related. It was a long day, and my knees hurt, and it would be late before I was home; I certainly did not want to stay at Granny's again.

A couple of weeks later I got a notification from the AACA, saying that the Lagonda had won a National First at Hershey! This was what I had had my heart set on since I began the project; I was tired of getting seconds. Seconds were not something that my professional career had prepared me for. But I hadn't really believed it was possible. There is a well known phenomenon called the impostor syndrome — the feeling many successful people have that they are impostors who will be uncovered at any moment. This is probably part of that — the feeling deep inside that I am really a Second kind of guy, and that this will be made clear by my never getting a First. Of course, the rational part of my head knows that this is not consistent with the evidence, but that doesn't seem to help a lot. I was delighted. They sent a brass and enamel plaque to be mounted on the car.

We had to get to the bottom of these brakes. My friend John Pinner put me in touch with a man who worked for the Ferodo company, which had made the brake lining used in the original Lagonda. He admitted in confidence that, try as they might, they had never been able to get the same coefficient of friction out of the modern brake lining after they removed the asbestos. He said that he had a roll of the original brake lining out in his garage, and he offered me enough to reline my brakes. With the new lining, the brakes were much better, though only by comparison.

Pretty as it is, the Lagonda suffered from being an orphan. Normally, after a car is designed, it goes through a shakedown period before it is offered for sale. In the case of the 2.6 liter Lagonda, this period had coincided with the financial difficulties of the company. This meant that the shaking down had been rudimentary at best. The brakes, in particular, had never been properly sorted out. The shop manual does mention that the brakes must be relined with the specific Ferodo lining, or their performance will suffer. This suggests that the factory was aware of the problem but felt that the use of the Ferodo lining improved them enough to get by.

The next fall, the Lagonda Club USA had a rally in honor of the 100th anniversary of the founding of the Lagonda Motor Company. The rally was to be held at Springfield, Ohio, the birthplace of the founder of the company. Lagonda is a corruption of the Indian name for a creek outside Springfield, Ough Ohonda.

The founder had gone to England to become an opera singer just before the turn of the century; when that didn't work out, he tried manufacturing steam yachts; that also was not a success, so he tried bicycles; failure again, so he tried cars, which were just coming into vogue. That worked. Cornell finds that the successful people who donate money to its endowment have generally failed three or four times, so the founder of Lagonda was typical.

Participants were to come from all over the United States and from England. Arrangements were being made for English participants to be taken in US cars to Springfield. Several routes were planned, to lead participants from New England and the Middle Atlantic states to meet in western Pennsylvania, whence they would proceed together to Springfield. The routes were all by easy stages of 200 miles per day, with attractive stops each night with the possibility of good meals.

This sounded very nice, and I signed up. I was asked to arrange the stopover in western Pennsylvania.

My wife, Jane, taught in the Statler School of Hotel and Restaurant Administration at Cornell for over 20 years, teaching restaurant reviewing (among other things), and was for several years a restaurant reviewer for DiRoNA, Distinguished Restaurants of North America, a joint endeavor of the North American Hotel and Restaurant Association and American Express. As a result we have a lot of contacts among food and wine people. Using these contacts, which led to a wine merchant in the region whom I had known some years before in a wine-tasting society, I found a nice inn in Chautauqua that served gourmet meals. I reserved a block of rooms. It seemed that we were all set for a lovely few days in the fall.

To my horror, as the time for the rally approached, one after another participant dropped out until I found that I would be alone in Chautauqua. Well, I like being alone, and at least I would get a good meal. Of the British participants, the only one left was the official representative of the owners' club.

When I embarked on the trip, it was the time of year for the show at Hershey, so of course it poured, and I still had not figured out what was the matter with my wipers. I also found that my windscreen leaked slightly, so that as I drove I had to keep mopping with a rag to prevent the water from dripping on the nice woodwork.

The inn in Chautauqua was harder to find than I had thought, and it was late and dark and pouring when I pulled up. The thought of the gourmet meal sustained me. I went in and registered. As I turned to go up to my room, I asked what time dinner would be. The woman of the couple who owned the inn pointed out that I had not made a reservation for a place at dinner, that the dining room was full, and that I would have to eat somewhere down the road.

The next morning I stopped at a hardware store before leaving town and bought a caulking gun, a tube of silicone caulk, and a roll of masking tape. Then I stopped at a supermarket for a potato. I pulled into the forecourt of a garage that was open and asked if they minded if I did some minor repairs there. They were gracious, and I masked off the windshield and laid a crude bead of caulk on the edge of the leaking seal. Then I cut the potato into fingers, and used the wet edge of one of the fingers to squeegee the caulk into a respectable, tiny and nearly invisible bead. I stripped off the tape, and we were ready to go. In a perfect world, I would have let it dry a while before subjecting it to air pressure, but the world is not perfect. At least it had stopped raining during the night.

Crossing Ohio I was on the truck route. The pounding of the 18-wheelers had destroyed the roadbed and the Lagonda went ka-thump, ka-thump, ka-thump as we went along. This constant thumping caused the latches on the convertible top to open. If both sides had come completely undone at the same time, and I had not noticed, the wind would have caught the top and flipped it open and torn it off the car. Fortunately the latch is fail-safe, so that even when undone it still remains hooked over a pin. This fail-safe feature saved the top dozens of times, as I noticed the top bobbing up and down against the loose hooks, my attention having been distracted by a passing 18-wheeler.

I got to Springfield without incident. Despite the many dropouts, there was still a respectable representation of Lagondas through the ages. There was not one of every model that Lagonda had produced, but there was at least one from each period. Two distinguished older cars had been brought in on trailers, one from Alaska and the other from California. Our cars were washed by a local church group. We precessed in the cars to a fairground (next to the eponymous creek) where the cars were placed on display in tents; speeches were made about hands across the sea, and plaques awarded to the representatives of the UK Club.

We shared the fairgrounds with the Steam Threshermen's Association, and while the crowds looked at the Lagondas, we looked at the steam-driven farm equipment. Much of the equipment was running; laborious efforts were being made to start what was not by heavy sweating men in bib overalls.

For lunch, they took us by bus to view a museum and restoration facility nearby. A local contractor who had made a great deal of money, and who loved old cars, had a stunning collection of distinguished cars from the early thirties. Rolls-Royce, Delage, Packard, and Duesenberg are names that stick in my mind, but essentially every distinguished make of the period was represented. The cars were splendidly restored. When the contractor found that he could not get restoration work done of the quality he wanted, he helped to found a restoration facility nearby. We toured that also. They were prepared to design and build a custom period body, if, for example, you came across a distinguished bodyless chassis. Of course, they did panel beating and had various specialized machines to hammer out things like spare wheel covers. I remarked to the young man demonstrating one of these machines that I did similar things, on a very small scale, and by hand; he said that he had been taught his craft in that way "by an old gentleman like you." I am now using this facility for my plating, and they do wonderful work. This facility does all the restoration for the contractor, but they are also available to the general public. I suspect that the demand for restoration work of this quality is probably not sufficient to sustain the staff of such a facility, and they are probably subsidized by the contractor, God bless him. They do perfectly beautiful work; they are a treasure. They had just finished a splendid Delage from the late thirties, a convertible in moss green with a louvered hood. One could imagine racing down the N7 between rows of *platanes* on the way to Nice, the headlamps cutting swaths through the pouring rain on a late autumn night, a beautiful woman on the passenger seat.

The contractor and his wife served us an excellent lunch at tables placed among the beautiful cars, and gave us a little talk about his experiences with the museum and restoration facility.

Being bused back to the fairground at the end of the day was a bit of a comedown. We had dinner with the Steam Threshermen — hamburgers, potato salad, baked beans. Classic Midwestern fairground food. I left in the morning to drive back to Ithaca, but the meeting was to continue through that day, with a reception at the country club that night.

I had made arrangements to stop at the inn at Chautauqua on the way back, and had been careful to reserve for dinner. However, I found the 200 miles per day a bit leisurely and wanted to cut a day from the itinerary. I called to change my reservations, to find that I would now land in Chautauqua on the owners' day off, and no dinner would be available. I decided that I was doomed.

I must say, however, that aside from the leaking windscreen, I had no trouble with the car. The car of the organizer, which was carrying the British guests from New England, had no end of trouble, sprinkling the highway with bits of the starter at one point. The passengers had to dismount and search the highway, hats in hand, looking for the vital nuts and bolts. I should count my blessings.

Chapter 14

Bentley

WITH THE COMPLETION OF THE Lagonda I was again at a loose end. My Toyota truck had some 130,000 miles on it and badly needed rings and bearings, a clutch and a water pump. Since my intensive care ward was presently unoccupied, I pulled the engine and did all that, and reconditioned the head. At the same time, I got a pair of previously owned doors from our local junkyard and a pair of Taiwanese front fenders. I took off the bed, which was rapidly dissolving with rust and was an eyesore, and built a new one from pressure-treated lumber. I put on new front and back bumpers from J.C. Whitney, and even chipped the rust off the frame and painted it with black Hammerite. Finally, I gave the sheet metal parts a fresh coat of cream enamel. It was beautiful (after a manner of speaking). I tried to remind myself this was *not* a restoration.

I needed another project. Considering my age, this might well be my last project. I had thought for many years that I should try, at least once, a Rolls-Royce or a Bentley, just to see whether the mystique is justified. I had heard all the myths over the years, from people who had restored all kinds: some said that Rolls-Royces were not much different from, and in some ways not as well made as, other makes, while others said that every aspect was unique and wonderful.

But first, I had to get rid of a car. I have storage space for two cars, and space to work on one. Something would have to go. This decision was as painful for me as selling one of my children down river into white slavery. I decided that the Armstrong Siddeley 346 was the only candidate. I couldn't sell the Lagonda, which was too freshly done. The Star was too nice to drive.

I advertised the 346 in *Hemmings* and in the house organ of the Antique Automobile Club of America, and on eBay. There were very, very few nibbles; nothing at all on eBay. Finally I got one phone call from a *Hemmings* reader. The man was in Mobile, Alabama, and wanted to know all about the car. I sent him pictures. In the meantime, I started to fix the inevitable little problems that had marred the appearance of the 346 during the ten years or so since the restoration had been finished.

The man from Mobile called again and again, and it was clear he was hooked. It turned out that he was the music director of a cathedral in Mobile and did not know much about cars, but evidently had fallen in love. He was prepared to pay my asking price, which I had set at the market value listed in *Thoroughbred and Classic Cars*. In order to get a bank loan, he needed paperwork on the car and its provenance and value, which I was happy to provide. Finally, payment and shipment were arranged. I finished the detailing of the car, and it was heartbreakingly beautiful.

The car transporter arrived just as hurricane Agnes arrived. North Carolina was under water. Ithaca was being whipped by heavy rain and high winds. The car was loaded just after dark in an atmosphere more appropriate to Heathcliff and the moors. The driver seemed very sympathetic, and we discussed the route he would have to take to avoid the flooding. My wife and I stood in the rain with tears in our eyes and waved goodbye to the beautiful car.

The 346 finally arrived in Mobile, apparently without incident, and I began getting phone calls from the new owner. On the one hand, he was absolutely delighted with the appearance of the car, but he had problems. It did not seem to run properly; it had developed various symptoms that were absolutely incomprehensible to me. I finally figured out that the new owner's knowledge of cars was so woefully lacking that I was not getting a straight story from him. He was misinterpreting things, drawing incorrect conclusions, and describing things incorrectly. In addition, he was apparently in the hands of a mechanic who either did not know what he was doing or more likely was taking the new owner for a ride, hoping for some lucrative work. When I sent the car down, the engine was essentially in perfect condition, and I knew nothing much could have happened to it in transit other than getting a little wet.

I kept getting phone calls weekly from the new owner, and we gradually sorted out the various symptoms, most of which slowly disappeared without specific treatment. I remember at one point he said he had been told that it had a bad rear wheel bearing that would have to be replaced. When the car went around a corner, it made a serious noise. I told him a wheel bearing problem was very unlikely, and that the most likely thing was that the fender skirt was rubbing on the tire, and needed to be bent a little. He could not believe this, since his mechanic had told him it was surely a wheel bearing. I convinced him to take off the fender skirt and drive the car around the block, and of course it no longer made the noise. He bent the skirt slightly, and the noise went away.

Although I had sent him detailed instructions on the proper use of the preselector gearbox, he had continual trouble with it, convinced that it needed to be dismantled and fixed. When I sent it, there was nothing the matter with it, and I strongly doubted that there was anything the matter with it now. I think he just was incapable of learning how to use it properly. I managed to keep him from turning it over to a mechanic to destroy, and we slowly got him trained so that complaints about the gearbox gradually stopped.

Eventually the phone calls and e-mails stopped, and I heaved a sigh of relief. All along, he had been very happy with the appearance of the car. He got comments in traffic all the time, and these really pleased him. Evidently it was now behaving well for him, too.

Then one day I got another call. He was entering bankruptcy and was selling the car to his lawyer. I was speechless. I have heard nothing since. I still regret selling the 346, but I had no choice.

I had been looking for another car, and I saw one advertised in *Hemmings Motor News*. It was a Mk. VI Bentley of 1951, 4.25 liters, the standard steel saloon. It was in my price range, which is to say, cheap.

After the war, Rolls-Royce decided that they had to rationalize their product line, and they decided to offer a mass-produced steel body, made by Pressed Steel, which also made bodies for several less prestigious makers. They did not make a big fuss about this, because they did not feel it would be very good for their image. However, these bodies by Pressed Steel were much cheaper and better made than the coach-built bodies Rolls-Royce had made in house before the war. They still did all the painting and coach-trimming themselves.

These early postwar cars were just about at the price minimum; Rolls-Royce and Bentley cars either earlier or more recent were substantially more expensive. I thought the lines of the Mk. VI were quite interesting. The Rolls and the Bentley are almost identical except for the radiator shell. The Rolls engine has only one carburetor, as opposed to the Bentley's two, and the Rolls has a less aggressive camshaft. I much prefer the look of the Bentley radiator shell to the Rolls.' The initial purchase price of the Bentley is virtually the same as that of the Rolls (something like £200 difference for the radiator shell), but the resale value is very different, with the Rolls demanding much more than the Bentley. For this reason sales of new Bentleys fell off seriously in later years, and the company finally took steps to make the Bentley more attractive, to counter the trend. However, this meant that the price of a Mk. VI Bentley was substantially less than that of a Silver Wraith, the equivalent Rolls.

The Mk. VI was down in a suburb of Easton, Pennsylvania, just west of the New Jersey–Pennsylvania line. I called and made arrangements to see it. It is only about a three hour drive one way, and I could be down and back in a day.

The address was in a development of ranch-style houses. I knocked on the door, which was answered by the wife. The husband was out on the road, but he had his cell phone and she contacted him. He would be back in just a few minutes; in the meantime, she opened the garage door and invited me to look at the car.

The car appeared to be approximately complete, although it was a little hard to tell. It had been partially dismantled, and many parts were in boxes and tubs in the back. Someone had been doing body work on it, consisting mostly (as far as I could see) of the use of body filler. I suspected there was not much under the filler. It was clear that the sills were severely rusted, as well as the trunk floor. However, most of the chrome appeared to be present. It was missing its back seat. The interior trim had been removed, or was hanging in shreds. The mechanical parts were all there.

The husband showed up with a friend. It transpired that the car had originally been bought by someone else in the neighborhood, who had begun to restore it. He had gotten it running, and had taken it out on the local streets, only to discover that it didn't have any brakes and that the generator didn't work. In attempting to rebuild the engine, he had found that a set of bearing shells was in the neighborhood of $700, and that had deterred him from making further progress. The car had sat in his back yard out in the weather for an unknown period — perhaps several years — and he had finally sold it to these guys, who were anxious to prevent further deterioration.

It was really a parts car, just at the limit of restorability. However, this is the kind of challenge that I like. This car in reasonable condition, registered and inspected, but needing restoration, was worth perhaps $12,000. I offered them $3,500. They looked at each other and said that they had a hundred more than that in it. I upped my offer to $3,600, and they accepted it.

I was very happy on the drive home. I am a romantic at heart, and I fantasize a lot. I was not yet aware of all the problems that this vehicle had.

When I got home, I arranged for a roll-back to pick up the Mk. VI and bring it to Ithaca. When the truck pulled up in front of the house, the

The Bentley as it arrived. Some of the missing parts (e.g., the grille and radiator shell) are in the back.

driver was a slender young woman. I wondered how we were going to get the 4200 pound car into the barn. I asked as delicately as I knew how whether she had picked the car up alone, and she nearly bit my ears off. Just then a car pulled up, and a man got out and started giving her grief, asking whether she was really capable of handling that great big truck all by herself, and on and on. Her jaw was firmly clenched when she introduced me to her brother. Fortunately, he agreed to help push the Bentley into the barn, and we managed to get it in in one smooth swoop.

I now went over what I had bought with a fine-tooth comb, making lists of what I had and what was missing. The missing list was pretty long, including a bumper and a back seat. I looked through *Hemmings Motor News* and found the name of Oregon Crewe Cutters, specializing in used Bentley and Rolls-Royce parts. I faxed them my list of needs. In the fullness of time (they evidently have little competition) they faxed me back a price list, and I went into cardiac arrest. My little list was worth over $6,000. We needed another solution.

In the meantime, I had joined the Rolls-Royce Owners' Club, which is a US group. In addition, I had joined the Rolls-Royce Enthusiasts' Club

The rear view. All that filler was applied over rust.

and the Bentley Drivers' Club, both UK organizations. All of these offer shop manuals, parts lists, collections of service bulletins, owner's manuals and so forth. The R-REC also offers factory records. I sent away for all of these.

The RROC maintains a website for technical discussions. I sent a message asking for suggestions of how I might obtain the parts I needed at a more reasonable price. I got a reply from someone I already knew, a wealthy hotel owner in Curaçao who maintains a house in Ithaca (among other places) and sometimes spends the summer here. He owns a large stable of beautiful cars, including several vintage Bentleys. He suggested I get in touch with a man named Mike who lived a couple of miles from my house, and who was also restoring a Mk. VI Bentley.

I made arrangements to visit Mike, who turned out to be about my age. He is an engineer who had founded and run a small company, which he had sold at a handsome profit when he retired. He was restoring a coach-built convertible. He had bought a parts car, a standard steel saloon like mine. He would not be needing most of the body parts from the parts car, since the convertible body was quite different. He was happy to sell me a one-third interest in the parts car, with the understanding that he had first call on any part. The parts car had nearly everything I would need to complete mine, except for a rear bumper. The arrangement has worked out

The dashboard.

beautifully. In addition, we have been able to exchange information and tools, and to hold each other's hands when problems arise. His restoration is several years ahead of mine. However, I am catching up, because I put in a lot more hours per week than he does.

As I began to dismantle the Bentley, I found some appalling things. In the first place, the previous owner had evidently sandblasted the entire car without dismantling anything, and then spray-painted the entire underside with POR-15, the isocyanate that seals rust. The net result was that sand was in the suspension and running gear, and would have destroyed the car if it had been on the road. Fortunately, it was in no condition to run. The sandblasting was very sloppy and the chassis was nothing like clean, but the very tough POR-15 was all over everything, filling screw slots and sealing threads. In addition, it covered everything that was supposed to be plated, all the bolt heads and wiring and tubing clips. The engine had been painted grey (it was supposed to be shiny black), and the firewall had been painted black (it was supposed to be nickel plated). The radiator had been filled up with tap water, which had been allowed to evaporate over a number of years. Since the head was aluminum and the block iron, considerable electrolytic corrosion had taken place. The radiator was as full of holes as a Swiss cheese. The block was filled with a fine three-dimensional network

The engine, which doesn't look bad from the outside except for the color.

of white threads, presumably some aluminum compound that had grown dendrites as the water evaporated. My heart sank. I hoped the engine could be saved. Most of the corrosion had probably taken place in the head, since aluminum corrodes sacrificially relative to iron. I certainly had my work cut out for me.

We still have in Ithaca an old-fashioned radiator man. He is officially retired, but he still has all his equipment (and his marbles), and he will take on interesting jobs. I pulled the radiator and took it down to him. To my horror, I discovered that he had moved in with his son, who runs a garage, and had closed up his shop behind his former house. I was afraid I was out of luck. However, I went out to the son's garage and presented my problem. He said his dad was still taking a few jobs and would be happy to do the Bentley radiator. Of course, it had to be re-cored, and of course a core of the original type was unavailable, which may have been a good thing. We did manage to find a core that was nearly the right thickness. I impressed on him that the core had to slip into a cradle, and that it was vitally important that it end up the right width and height, since it also held up the front of the hood. Fortunately, when it came back, it was perfect.

The front suspension was a mess. Bentley does tend to pick engineering solutions that are unnecessarily complicated and prone to failure. It takes creativity to imagine an elegantly simple, fail-safe solution. I have a friend who has a saying that he uses like a mantra: that anyone can design a water pump for a Rolls-Royce. All you have to do is make it of stainless, put in three shaft seals so that it cannot possibly leak, and to hell with the cost. To design a water pump for a Chevrolet, on the other hand, requires real creativity, because it has to be cheap to make and maintain, and be very reliable; the solutions suggested above are not an option. In fact, this is a canard, because the water pump on the Mk. VI is a very ordinary, simple, straightforward design, prone to corrosion and less well made than that on the Armstrong Siddeley Star. However, the sentiment is correct.

All the suspension bushings are rubber save one. That is the most vulnerable one, the lower outside bushing. That is a beautiful construction with two needle bearings that have to be assembled with a pair of forceps, needle by needle, placed in a bed of grease to hold them in place until the whole thing is slid together.

All the suspension points are lubricated by a Bijur chassis lubricator. This has a reservoir and a pump on the firewall, and very small brass tubing that goes to each suspension point, ending in drip plugs that meter oil into the points. The drip plugs are different sizes for each location. The pump is actuated by a pedal, and the driver is supposed to step on the pedal each time he gets into the car, and every 200 miles thereafter. I also had this system on the 1932 Nash, but there the pump was actuated by manifold vacuum. Bijur still makes this system for lubrication of large stationary factory machines, such as stamping presses. This system is fine as long as it is carefully maintained and religiously used. Otherwise, tubes get clogged, or crushed by jacking, careless mechanics, or accidents, or the wrong lubricant is put in the reservoir, or nothing at all, or it is not used, and suspension joints are starved of oil.

The front lower outer pivots had not seen oil for decades, and the beautiful needle bearing assembly was a solid block of rust in which individual needles were no longer discernible. I delicately dismantled them using a large sledge hammer and an acetylene torch. Because the Bentley is of interest to people with money, nearly everything needed for a restoration is available for a price. Since these lower outer suspension pivots are so vulnerable and prone to failure, a number of sources have replacements available, differing only in the extortionate prices quoted. There is a feeling, as with a yacht, that if you have to ask the price, you probably shouldn't be doing this restoration.

I admit that supplying parts to restorers is a labor of love. It is a hard way to make a living. Realistic pricing is absolutely essential if these vital people are to remain in business. Many owners' clubs supply parts at unrealistic prices, resulting in ultimate disaster. It takes a good accountant to price a reproduction part realistically, taking into account all market factors. The market is very small, and parts must often be held in inventory for decades. That said, there are certainly some examples of price gouging in the Rolls-Bentley parts business. There is, for example, one manufacturer of handmade body repair panels, in England. Everybody buys panels from this manufacturer. He is a member of a consortium of Rolls-Bentley restoration and maintenance providers, and they all offer the panels at the same prices. This is probably an example of price-fixing. The panels are expensive, but the pricing is fair, I believe. These things are hard to make. However, one US Rolls-Bentley restoration specialist offers these same panels at a price 2.5 times the price at the source. What is this, a fine old wine stocked in the cellar of an upscale restaurant? I import parts from the United Kingdom often enough to know that a factor of 2.5 is far in excess of any shipping costs.

At any rate, I bought beautiful new parts to restore the lower outer pivots, as well as the kingpins, and got all new rubber bushings for the other suspension points.

When the frame was stripped of all suspension and drivetrain parts, I repaired some sections on the side rails behind the rear axle, which had rusted through. Then I did the sensible thing, and sent it out to be sandblasted by a specialist. I have a friend who runs the Glenside Monument Company. He cuts inscriptions on tombstones using a sandblaster, and he has a very large one. He is an ex–drag racer and has a full shelf of trophies, so he is quite sympathetic to car guys. He is a cheerful, skinny, energetic, garrulous guy with a luxuriant moustache, and a son and daughter who are off to college. He is assembling a hot car in a period body as a wedding present for his son, though I think he may have to make one for himself when his son drives this one away. He agreed to take on the frame, on the proviso that he could subcontract it to his son, who was home from college and seriously in need of pocket money. He even provided pickup and delivery service in the truck in which he normally shifts gravestones. The son did a beautiful job — the frame came back absolutely clean, and with no sand anywhere.

I painted the beautiful clean frame with POR-15 again. However, this time it did not cover the things it was not supposed to cover. I did it with a brush, because special breathing apparatus is required if it is sprayed. Painting a frame with anything is a mess, because there are so many little nooks and crannies. Doing it with POR-15 is even worse, because this stuff has low viscosity and high surface tension, which makes it run everywhere, particularly down the brush handle. It cannot be gotten on the skin, unless you want to wear it for several weeks. When it is still just tacky, it should be top coated with a black semigloss ordinary frame paint, which means that the whole thing has to be done in one go. By the time you are at one end of the frame with your brush, going as fast as you can, with the POR-15 running down your arm, the other end has reached the slightly tacky stage and is ready to be sprayed. I loaded the gun and gave the whole thing four coats. It looked lovely. In a perfect world I probably should have filled the rust pits. There are heavy sanding primers that fill rust pits, and I could have sprayed the whole thing, and then sanded everything — and *then* started the routine with the POR-15 and the top coat. I am sorry; I love these cars, but not that much. As a result, the rear end of the frame has a roughened surface from the rust. The front end looks better — there was more grease up there, and consequently less rust.

When the engine block was stripped of all parts, I got out my pressure washer. The washer has a long wand that will reach through the holes in the deck down to the bottom of the water jacket. I was able to wash out all the strange white stuff as well as the accumulation of 50 years of rust particles in the bottom, leaving nothing loose, and a clean but rusted surface. I did this at the garage door, and afterward there was a moraine of rust particles on the driveway.

I took the block and head out to one of the few remaining local machine shops. This is run by a bright and interested young man. He does pretty well rebuilding tractor and truck engines for the local farmers, and keeping their cars on the road. He is involved in ultralight aircraft, and one end of his shop is taken up by various aircraft under construction. He had just purchased a very high-tech balancing machine and gave me a special price to do detailed balancing on the Bentley engine, in addition to the other work I wanted done.

I had obtained a set of pistons, pins and rings from England. These were of the type that had been used when the engine was first made. They were new old stock, and had been sitting on a shelf somewhere for 50 years. They came packed in heavy Cosmoline, as though they had been intended for shipment to the tropics. The boxes did not carry a Rolls-Royce logo but instead had an Austin logo. I was quite perplexed for some time, until I discovered that Austin had manufactured a sort of SUV (called something like a Cubby or Chubby) using the Rolls-Royce engine design, which they manufactured under license.

The crankshaft had at one time been reground to the limit. The crank was in terrible condition, and would have required removal of as much again, which was out of the question. I went to the Roll-Royce owners' club online chat room and indicated my needs. Almost immediately, I received a reply from someone in Virginia, who said that he believed he had a crank in his barn, and he would go and look. After careful measurement, we determined that it was the correct crank, that it had not been ground, and that it would clean up with a relatively light grinding. I made an elaborate plywood crate and sent it to Virginia. In due course I got the crate back, this time with the crank inside.

I had the shop machine nearly every surface of the engine to remove the wear and accommodate the new parts. When I stood bail to get the engine out of stir, I found that the cleaning process had gone through the head in a couple of places, and the shop had had to weld in patches before machining the head. This should have been a warning, but it was already too late.

The engine had originally been covered in high gloss black baked enamel. I coated all the appropriate places with a high gloss black engine paint, after painfully masking the parts that should not be painted. The hardest part was the Bentley logo on the valve cover, which is supposed to be left in unpainted aluminum, to contrast nicely with the black.

The engine was reassembled. Before I could put it back in the chassis, I had to rebuild the transmission, since this supports the rear of the engine. That is, the engine and the transmission form a sort of bridge — they are bolted together, and the rear of the transmission and the front of the engine are supported.

The most annoying thing about working on this car is the difficulty of getting parts rapidly. Where any other manufacturer would use an O-ring, which is universally obtainable, Rolls-Royce makes a special rubber ring with a different cross section that can only be obtained from Rolls-Royce. It does the job no better, and results in both expense and delay. Every nut has a tab washer locking it in place. Many manufacturers have found that these are unnecessary and represent a sort of compulsion. They have to be obtained from Rolls-Royce and cannot be reused. I have discovered how to make many of these tab washers, at least in the larger sizes. In some cases in exasperation I have used Lock-Tite, an anaerobic glue which is placed on the threads and acts as a chemical lock-washer. The bearings in the transmission, most of which showed wear, were nearly all special in some way, so that they could not be obtained from a local jobber. These are not used by anybody else, and consequently are inordinately expensive and difficult to get. In addition, in nearly half the cases, the wrong parts were sent, and had to be sent back. I find this absolutely maddening.

In any event, eventually the transmission was together and joined to the engine. This is like assisting in the mating of locomotives—the input shaft of the transmission has to be delicately introduced into the center of the flywheel and the transmission gently moved forward until the splines engage the clutch disk, and finally the holes in the flange are aligned, and then the whole thing bolted together. This is not helped by the fact that the transmission is too heavy for one person to lift, or at least, to lift and simultaneously maneuver delicately. This process is not quite as bad as installing a VW engine, which has to be done the same way — there the transmission is in the car, and the engine is even larger than the Bentley transmission. I learned some tricks that eventually made that routine, and this sort of thing is now fairly straightforward. I did enlist the help of a stonemason who was repairing our back garden to help me carry the transmission to the engine.

When the engine was installed in the chassis, and all the auxiliaries installed, it was time to try starting it, always an exciting time. I filled up the cooling system with coolant in preparation. From the left front corner of the cylinder head, a fine steady stream of coolant squirted out horizontally, hitting the floor some three or four feet from the engine. It was reminiscent of the famous Manneken Pis in Brussels. There was evidently a perforation in the head that we had missed. I drained out the coolant and tried plugging the hole. I drilled it out, trying to find sounder material that could take a thread to hold a screw. The hole got larger and larger, but the material remained paper thin. When I reached a quarter inch, I stopped. I suppose I could have cut the wall away until I reached thicker material (if I ever did), welded in a patch, had the head remachined (because the welding heat would distort it) and hoped, but it seemed to me likely that if there was one thin perforated place, there were probably others close to coming through.

Fortunately, the parts car had a cylinder head that was far less corroded. It had evidently been run on antifreeze with corrosion inhibitors. I went over to Mike's house and pulled the head from the parts car, and I started over. The new head was lovely, and when it was reconditioned, I installed it, and the engine started and ran beautifully.

Usually the rear axle of an old car is the one part that does not need to be rebuilt. I can only conclude that they are uniformly overdesigned. I had had to rebuild the Lagonda rear axle because the thrust washers were worn out. The Bentley rear axle also required attention — there was perhaps 45 degrees of play in the propeller shaft, indicating that something was very wrong.

The Bentley axle is not put together like other axles (of course not!). It is held together by dozens of square-headed bolts, which are nearly impossible to remove. One side holds an enormous spring in place, and must be taken apart under a hydraulic press to keep the spring from going through the ceiling when the last bolt is removed. The other side is held in place by a uniquely Bentley inside-out left-hand nut. Fortunately Mike had made a tool for undoing this.

When I finally got inside and cleaned everything up, I found that the bearings and thrust washers had to be replaced, but the gears looked pretty good. I sent away for washers of the required thickness. Word came back that the stock had become depleted over the years, and the sizes I needed were no longer available. I had to make do with thicker washers, which I ground down by hand on a piece of sandpaper. I pushed the washers around and around, stopping every ten circuits or so to measure the thickness. This kind of thing is very soothing for a slightly autistic person, but it did go on for a long time, and my hands were sore.

When it was time to reassemble the rear axle with all new bearings, the clearance of the ring and pinion had to be adjusted. The old-fashioned way to make this adjustment is to set the axle up the way you think it should be, take it apart and paint the tooth faces with Prussian blue (an artist's oil color that comes in a tube, and is a deep greenish blue), reassemble the axle and rotate it several times, and then dismantle it and examine the tooth faces. The Prussian blue will show where the teeth have been in contact, and old books give instructions on which adjustment to change to move the tooth contact to where it should be. This is tedious but relatively straightforward. It is a lot easier if the axle has an inspection cover on the back, so that the whole process can be done without dismantling the axle each time. With the Bentley axle, complete dismantling is necessary. If I were doing this for a living, I could probably have gotten it right in three complete cycles. I am afraid that I had to go through a dozen, mostly because I don't do this more than once a decade. Because of the wear on all the tooth faces, the play in the propeller shaft can just be felt. This is an enormous improvement on the previous state, and is probably better than any of my other cars.

It was time to assemble the rear brakes. The brake drums are finned on the outside. The previous owner had evidently had difficulty getting the brake drums off, and had used a large sledge, breaking most of the fins. I took my drums over to Mike's house and exchanged them for those from the parts car. I carefully cleaned and painted them, and tried to install them on my car. It was at this point that I discovered that they would not fit; there had evidently been a small change between the parts car and my car. The drums and the backing plates were incompatible. I verified in the parts book that the numbers had indeed changed, something I should have done before I cleaned up and painted my backing plates. I trudged back to the

All my chicks. Actually, the 346 had just been sold down the river, and would be picked up the next day.

parts car with my backing plates, and exchanged them with those from the parts car. At least these were in better condition.

The bolts and screws, and to some extent the nuts, that hold everything together on the frame are mostly particular to Rolls-Royce, and would be expensive to replace. The bolts are square-headed. This is one of Henry Royce's little compulsions. The excuse is that the hole for a square headed bolt can sometimes be placed against a surface so that the square head holds the bolt from turning, so that only one wrench is required. The relatively small number of times that this can be done certainly does not justify the increased expense.

Henry Royce also felt that normal nuts are not thick enough, and specified nuts 1.5 times the thickness of a standard SAE nut. Now, let me explain: the correct tightness of a nut on a bolt is determined by the tightness required to approach the yield strength of the bolt, the point at which the bolt begins to stretch. The thickness of an SAE nut is designed so that the nut will yield when the bolt yields. Making the nut 1.5 times as thick means that the bolt will yield first, and the nut will not. I fail to see the advantage.

However, there are certain nuts that are quite visible, and if they are not the Henry Royce specified nuts they do not look right: the cylinder head nuts and the nuts that hold the differential together are examples of these. All in all, I sent off about 500 fasteners to the platers. I found a plater who would undertake to remove grease, paint and rust and plate the fasteners with white zinc for something like 40 cents a fastener.

Another Rolls-Royce specialty is the use of half nuts. These are half the thickness of a normal SAE nut. When a bolt and nut are entirely in shear, it is not necessary to stress the bolt nearly to its yield, and a thinner nut will do just fine. Most automobile manufacturers would not dream of increasing their costs by maintaining an inventory of half nuts, and training personnel to install them in certain places but not in others; the cost of a half nut is slightly lower than the cost of a full nut, but not enough to compensate. They also save a little weight, but not much, and there is no evidence that Rolls-Royce cared very much about the weight of this vehicle.

Inevitably, some things that would need plating were not sent off with the main shipment of fasteners, and I had to go into the plating business myself. Eastwood supplies a plating kit that allows one to plate small parts with a tin-zinc compound. I have a built-in suspicion of these things, having sent away for many such things when I was a teenager only to receive something deeply disappointing that could never be made to work. I remember in particular a welding setup that was a disaster. In any event, the Eastwood plating arrangement has worked quite well, and I have done perhaps ten percent of the total collection of small parts myself.

The tiny brass tubes of the Bijur chassis lubrication system were cleaned, repaired or replaced. Since Bijur still exists and still makes lubrication systems for factories, tubing is available. They even sell internal parts for the drip plugs (which meter the oil), and you can get little plastic bags of tiny springs, tiny felt plug filters and tiny brass plates. Mike had sent for these, and with his guidance and these parts I managed to dismantle and repair some of my drip plugs. Some, however, were irreversibly choked. Fortunately, there is a company in England that makes new ones (primarily for a more upscale clientele — the owners of Silver Wraiths and other earlier Rolls-Royces). When I was all done, and the system was bled (just like a braking system), I pumped the pedal and oil dripped gently from a dozen places. It is important that no point have much less resistance than the others, because then it will get all the oil and the others will starve.

The firewall needed to be plated with matte nickel. I built an elaborate packing case for it and sent it to Ohio to the elegant restoration facility I had visited when I drove the Lagonda out. They did a lovely job. They are not cheap, but they do very nice work. I also had them plate the various tubes and other pieces on the engine — the starter housing, for instance, is plated in matte nickel.

Finally, the chassis was finished. I strapped a plastic milk case upside down to the frame so that I could sit and steer, and backed the chassis out into the driveway. Everything behaved as it should — the rear axle was silent, the brakes worked, the steering was fine, the transmission shifted properly, and the clutch worked. There were a few small oil leaks, but nothing serious.

I am just beginning the body. As usual, the bottom six inches are essentially gone. Most of this is attributable ultimately to drainage from the sunroof and the cowl ventilator. Drains are plugged by leaf debris, they rust away, and rubber connectors perish (as the Brits say), dumping water where it does not belong.

In compensation for all

A joint Christmas present from my son and my wife. The supporting ironwork was done by one of Chris' friends from Putney, Jonathan Hertz. The car is the 1954 Armstrong Siddeley 346 Sapphire. This is the barn in Ithaca where I work on the cars.

this rot, the door structure appears to be in reasonable condition.

Healy Brothers in the UK has handmade repair panels for all the sill (rocker panel) and fender sections. The sills run along the sides below the doors. Like all sills, the panels that close the front and back ends are exposed to the slop sprayed up by the wheels. Eventually these panels rust through, and then the slop goes right into the sills, where it takes a long time to dry up. All the while it is wet, it is rotting the structure.

At the moment, I am slowly working my way along the right side of the car. The very front of the sills is rotted away, and this is not a panel that Healy Brothers supplies. I do enjoy fabricating these panels. I could have fabricated the inner and middle sill panels, which Healy Brothers provided. Over the years I have accumulated a considerable number of sheet-metal working tools, but the outer panel is beyond my modest capabilities—it requires equipment I don't have yet. In any event, I decided I would have plenty to do fabricating the panels that Healy Brothers does not supply.

I have rebuilt the lower back corner of the rear seat pan, and the back of the door sill. There is now something to hang the sill panels from, and I can begin welding in the Healy Brothers panels. So far, I have only fitted them, to make sure everything lines up properly. Since the body is off the frame, and high up in the air to make working on it easier, I have to be sure that the body mounting points are where they are supposed to be, so the body will fit when it is lowered onto the chassis.

When the sills are reconstructed, I will start on the trunk floor and the rear fenders. There are several holes that must be patched: these are from water that came in through the wheel wells and ran down the floor. The worst place is the well at the very back of the floor, which extends right across the body, intended for tools of various sorts. There is not much left of that. Fortunately, Healy Brothers supplied this in three pieces. There will be plenty of small pieces to fabricate in addition.

* * *

I am retired now. I spend a couple of hours at the university in the morning, writing and doing academic housekeeping. I still have a few graduate students to finish up, and I am still editor of the *Annual Review of Fluid Mechanics*. At 11 o'clock every day I go over to the gym and work out for an hour or so. Then I have lunch and read the *New York Times*. Sometimes I doze off for a half hour. Then I go home. It is then about 2:30 or 3:00. I go out to the barn and work on uncle Bentley (from the Alan Sherman record *My Son the Folk Singer*, sung to the tune of *Frère Jacques*, "...How's your uncle Bentley? Feeling better ment'ley? That's nice too, that's nice too..." which should be sung with glottal stops replacing the "t"s).

I listen to National Public Radio the whole time. It is very peaceful and satisfying listening to Bach or Mozart and fabricating bits and pieces that (for the most part) fit pretty well. On Saturdays I get to listen to the opera. Sometimes it is difficult to bear, when the opera is something like Billy Budd, but there is compensation when it is something like *The Magic Flute* or *Così fan tutte*.

I have worked on cars all my life — my life has been all of a piece in this respect, and I can put myself back to age 16 very easily. I am glad that

I have acquired a lot of both manual and life skills that the 16-year-old did not have, and in all respects I am much happier than he was, but I am fond of him. I still try to cut corners in ways that are not recommended, and sometimes it works. I think this is the same thing I do professionally — someone in research does not always accept the received wisdom, and wants to try a little something different. In any case, professionally or out in the barn, I want to make something that works and is attractive; and if it is clever and a little different, all the better. For me, that has always been the kick.

Index